A HEART AS WIDE
AS THE WORLD

BOOKS BY SHARON SALZBERG

A Heart As Wide As the World:
Stories on the Path of Lovingkindness

Lovingkindness: The Revolutionary Art of Happiness

Voices of Insight

A HEART AS WIDE AS THE WORLD

Stories on the Path of Lovingkindness

Sharon Salzberg

SHAMBHALA
Boston & London
1999

Shambhala Publications, Inc.
Horticultural Hall
300 Massachusetts Avenue
Boston, Massachusetts 02115
www.shambhala.com

Permission has been granted to reprint material from the
following sources: From *Rilke's Book of Hours*, translated by
Anita Barrows and Joanna Macy, © 1996 by Anita Barrows
and Joanna Macy, reprinted by permission of Riverhead
Books; from *Tao Te Ching*, by Stephen Mitchell, © 1988 by
Stephen Mitchell, reprinted by permission of
HarperCollins; from *Dialogues with a Modern Mystic*, by
Andrew Harvey and Mark Matousek, © 1994 by Andrew
Harvey and Mark Matousek, reprinted by permission of
Quest Books; from *The Spring of My Life*, by Kobayashi Issa,
translated by Sam Hamill, © 1997 by Sam Hamill, reprinted
by permission of Shambhala Publications. An earlier version
of "Faith—to Place the Heart Upon" appeared in *Tricycle:
The Buddhist Review*, vol. VI, no. 2.

14 13 12 11 10 9 8 7
Printed in the United States of America
⊗ This edition is printed on acid-free paper that meets the
American National Standards Institute Z39.48 Standard.
♻ Shambhala Publications makes every effort to print on recycled
paper. For more information please visit www.shambhala.com.
Distributed in the United States by Random House, Inc.,
and in Canada by Random House of Canada Ltd

The Library of Congress catalogues the hardcover edition
of this book as follows:
Salzberg, Sharon.
    A heart as wide as the world: stories on the path of
    lovingkindness / Sharon Salzberg.—1st ed.
        p. cm.
    ISBN 978-1-57062-340-0 (cloth: alk. paper)
    ISBN 978-1-57062-428-5 (pbk.)
    1. Religious life—Buddhism. I. Title.
BQ5395.S25 1997   97-16985
294.3'444—dc21   CIP

IT IS COMPASSION that removes the heavy bar, opens the door to freedom, makes the narrow heart as wide as the world. Compassion takes away from the heart the inert weight, the paralyzing heaviness; it gives wings to those who cling to the lowlands of self.

—NYANAPONIKA THERA

Contents

Acknowledgments

I AM FOREVER GRATEFUL to His Holiness the Dalai Lama of Tibet, Aung San Suu Kyi of Burma, and all of my teachers, many of whose stories appear on these pages.

I would like to thank Sam Bercholz, who suggested I write another book, and Peter Turner, who made it real in the beginning, in the middle, and at the end.

The direction of this book was inspired by several important conversations, most notably with Alice Walker. Ongoing dialogues about spirituality and social action with Tara Bennett-Goleman, Mirabai Bush, Gary Cohen, Ram Dass, Carol Densmore, Amy Elizabeth Fox, Joseph Goldstein, Dan Goleman, Paul Gorman, Enid Gorman, Colin Greer, Joan Halifax, Charlie Halpern, Susan Halpern, Kedar Harris, and Jai Lakshman have changed my understanding in many ways.

Shoshana Alexander's visionary and editorial direction on the book were essential; plus, to whatever degree I am learning how to write, it is because she is teaching me. I also want to thank Kate Wheeler for revealing to me the point of some of my stories; and David Berman for so very many things, among them: telling me the middle path was like a fractal, turning out to be a computer genius, and staying up most of the night to make the disk. Also Hal Ross for the same late night, for turning out to be a wonderful editor, and for having a beautiful sense of service throughout.

Many people have helped me in significant ways during this period of writing, including: Seymour Boorstein, Amy Schmidt, Martha Ley, Sarah Doering, Sunanda Markus, Chris Desser, Anne Millikin, and John Friend. Eric McCord offered great service in clarifying text and creating a sequence to my flow of ideas. More people than can possibly be named helped in searching for a title for the book, but especially Steve Armstrong and Myoshin Kelley. There are friends named in my stories, including Joseph Goldstein, Kamala Masters, and Sylvia Boorstein, who gave me permission to write about them. Stories also appear about other, unnamed friends, the legion of which includes, but is not limited to: Susan Harris, Maggie Spiegel, Gina Thompson, David Berman, Ram Dass, Kate Wheeler, Catherine Ingram, Daeja Napier, Ashley Napier, Wayne Muller, Larry Rosenberg, Ann Buck, Mitch Kapor, and Meg Quigley. It is wonderful to be able to share this lifetime with all of them.

Introduction

FROM MY EARLIEST DAYS of Buddhist practice, I felt powerfully drawn to the possibility of finding a way of life that was peaceful and authentic. My own life at that time was characterized largely by fear and confusion. I felt separate from other people and from the world around me, and even oddly disconnected from my own experience. The world I experienced was sharply dualistic: self and other, us and them. This view increased my fear, which of course also increased my suffering.

Stepping onto the Buddhist path, I saw that it was possible to be free of feelings of separation and defensiveness— that one could live with a seamlessness of connection and an unbounded heart. The life of the Buddha embodied this. Wisdom and compassion consistently guided his actions, whether he was alone or with others, whether wandering through India or being still, whether teaching or silently meditating, whether with those who admired him or those who slandered him. There seemed to be no circumstance that limited his compassion; he truly had a heart as wide as the world.

The essence of the Buddha's teaching is that we all have this same capacity for compassion and for peace. This potential is not abstract or distant, not something available only to those who lived long ago in another land. A life of connection and authenticity can come completely alive for

us, now. We can make it our own. Discovering that our
hearts are indeed wide enough to embrace the whole world
of experience—both pleasurable and painful—is the basis of
the spiritual path, and with it comes an extraordinary freedom and happiness. This way of living is beautifully described by the poet Rilke:

> I live my life in widening circles
> that reach out across the world.
> I may not ever complete the last one,
> but I give myself to it.

As we give ourselves to the practice of mindfulness, wisdom, and compassion, our habitual patterns of attachment
and separation are seen for what they are: painful and unnecessary mistakes. This realization lifts the heaviness from
our hearts, so that we can encounter anything without
getting deeply lost in fear, anger, or clinging. We can encounter anybody without being engulfed by feelings of es-
trangement and separation. We can begin to live in a way
that enables our hearts to include rather than exclude, to
open rather than constrict, to go forward with the energy
of lovingkindness rather than be held back by the illusion
of separation. We can begin to live in a way that is commen-
surate with our own extraordinary potential—the potential
of being truly awake. This potential is the truth that lies at
the center of the Buddha's life and teaching. This truth is
also our truth. The unbounded heart of the Buddha can be
our own as well.

My hope is that this book may encourage you to bring
mindfulness, wisdom, and compassion to life through practice, so that you may learn that your own heart can become
as wide as the world. To paraphrase Rilke: you need only
give yourself to it.

Part One

The Spirit of Meditation

IN MEDITATION PRACTICE we explore the ways we relate to our own experiences and to our motivations for change. We look at the degree of concentration, mindfulness, and love that we bring to bear on whatever may be happening in our lives. Our efforts in meditation are directed toward opening, toward knowing what we feel, toward remaining awake to the suffering and joy we encounter. This is meditation as a way of life, a way of recapturing our lives so we can delight in the integrity, joy, and peace that arise from understanding the truth of who we are.

"I Have What You Need"

IN THE OLD CITY section of Jerusalem, there is a wonderful open-stall marketplace. It is a place teeming with life—a deluge of sights and sounds and goods for sale. When I was teaching in Israel once, some friends and I went there. As we were walking down an alleyway, one of the merchants called out to me, "I have what you need!" I felt a thrill go through my entire body. "Wow, he has what I need." I stopped, turned around, and starting walking toward him. Then I thought, "Wait a minute. First of all, I don't need anything, and second, how would he know he has what I need?"

In many ways the world is calling out to us all of the time: "I have what you need! I have what you need!" In response, we internalize those voices into: "I need. I need something. I'm in a state of deficit, of deprivation." It's as though we turn into some sort of cartoon figure, with our eyes popping out of our heads like they are on springs. "Where is it? Where is this thing I need?" Our arms extend, reaching out. The fingers flex, trying to grab and hold on to one object or another. Our heads rigidly fix in the direction of the object of desire, so as not to lose sight of it. Our bodies incline forward in anticipation. What an uncomfortable mess!

And yet we reach out time and time again, believing the voices. This movement, this constant reaching out, is felt as stress in the body and in the mind. "I have what you need," the voice tells us. "You don't have what you need. I have what you need." But what is it that we really need?

It is true that all beings want to be happy. We want to

feel at home in our own lives. We want to feel a part of something greater than our limited sense of who we are. We need an internal feeling of abundance, to be able to give to others. We need the fulfilling knowledge of our connection to all that lives, in order to love others. But in our habit of reaching out to satisfy our needs, we miss where our deepest satisfaction lies. A Tibetan text puts it like this: "Beneath the pauper's house there are inexhaustible treasures, but the pauper never realizes this, and the treasures never say, 'I am here.' Likewise, the treasure of our original nature, which is naturally pure, is trapped in ordinary mind, and beings suffer in poverty."

All of those voices lead us away from knowing that we already have what we need. When we practice meditation, we discover the treasure of our original nature. We learn to let go of that cacophony of voices shouting at us about our seeming poverty. We learn not to get caught in trying to reach out and grasp after things we never really needed to begin with.

When we practice meditation, we see that we can put down the burdens we have carried for so long. The poet Rumi says: "How long will we fill our pockets like children with dirt and stones? Let the world go. Holding it, we never know ourselves, never are airborne." When we practice meditation, we let go. We let go of our addictions to certain objects and experiences, let go of believing in those voices that call to us. We let go of our limited concepts of happiness and of who we are and what we need. Discovering the treasure of our original nature, we can be airborne. We can be free.

Coming Alive

NOT LONG AGO a friend of mine, who is normally a fairly healthy person, came down with a terrible case of pneumonia and was very close to dying. Sometime after his illness, I arrived home and found a message from him on my answering machine. Just as I was about to call him back, the phone rang. The caller happened to be a mutual friend. When I told her that I had to get off the phone to call our friend, she said in response, "Do you know that he almost died?" I told her that I did, and we ended the conversation so I could give him a call. Just as I hung up, the phone rang again, and it was another mutual friend. Once more, I told the caller I needed to get off the phone to speak to this friend who was sick, and she immediately said, "Well, do you know he almost died?"

When I finally managed to reach my friend, I said, "I think I may now expressly refer to you as 'He who almost died.'" My friend replied, 'Well, it's better than being known as 'He who almost lived.' "

"How do you mean that?" I asked. "Do you mean it like, 'He who almost escaped with his life but at the last moment didn't'?"

"No," he said, "More in the sense of how we can spend a lifetime almost living, rather than being truly alive."

Tragically, we may go through a great deal of our lives as if already dead. When we are unaware and disconnected, what could be a vibrant, vivid connection to all of life, with all of its pleasures and pains, becomes a sinking into death even while alive. Life becomes "virtual life." The Buddha said, "Those who are heedless, or unmindful, are as if dead already." Yet, some of us, feeling ourselves to be almost living, and profoundly wanting to be more fully awake, come to meditation practice—for to know ourselves, to be fully alive, we need to cultivate our power of awareness.

Awareness ignites a potent and vital energy in us. In Pali, which is the language of the original Buddhist texts, the term for this quality is *tejos*. The word has several meanings. It can mean heat, flame, fire, or light, and it conveys a sense of splendor and radiance and glory. *Tejos* refers to a bright energy, a strength, and a power that is luminous.

By practicing meditation, we bring forth some of this splendor, luminosity, and power into the activities of an ordinary day. We practice meditation to be aware, no matter what we are doing. And the deeper our awareness, the greater the luminosity. Through meditation we come to life, so as not to someday die as "one who almost lived."

For the Love of a Buddha

I WENT TO MY FIRST MEDITATION COURSE in Bodh-gaya, the village in India that has grown up around the tree under which the Buddha attained enlightenment. I was eighteen years old and, having recognized my confusion and unhappiness, I went to India to learn meditation. I was encumbered with conditioning from my childhood and my culture—self-hatred, self-judgment, the desire to be someone other than who I was. I think I secretly hoped to become entirely someone else through meditation practice.

Because I was one of the youngest Westerners there, out of curiosity someone asked me, "Why are you practicing meditation?" The first thing that came to my mind was an image of the Buddha in the main temple near the Bodhi tree, and I found myself saying, "I'm practicing so that I can have the love of a Buddha, so I can love people the way the Buddha did." I was actually startled to hear myself make that statement, but I knew it was emerging from a deep place within me.

By wanting to have the love of a Buddha, I was fundamentally seeking the ability to love myself, first of all, as I felt the Buddha would have—with clear seeing yet with undiminished compassion. In fact, the Buddha's teachings are the expression of that love, the emanation of his limitless compassion. Without sacrificing any clarity of perception, no being and no aspect of any being is left out of that space of love. This love is completely inclusive.

As I devoted myself to meditation practice, I repeatedly learned that I could not properly practice when motivated by self-hatred, self-condemnation, or tremulous grasping after some other, imaginary self. Spiritual practice motivated by these factors resembles an inner war, a brutal crusade for an ideal of goodness, with no mercy shown. I could only truly practice by incorporating my original motivation—to love myself and love others more perfectly. I found that remembering this brought forth the qualities of gentleness and spaciousness.

When self-judgment is present, we are committed to a path of avoidance and dissembling because the pain of judging whatever arises in the mind is just too difficult to bear. One year a friend of mine was sitting the annual three-month retreat at the Insight Meditation Society in Barre, Massachusetts. That particular year, our teacher Dipa Ma, whom we all loved and respected, visited during the course. This friend had been experiencing several very difficult days in the retreat, and he finally decided that what he needed to do was to leave the retreat, check into a motel, and watch a particular football game on television. So he did just that.

When he returned—I'm sure no happier than when he left—he was suddenly filled with guilt and tremendous self-judgment. He was also afraid to tell Dipa Ma what he had done. Day after day he anguished over it. "How can I tell her that I did this thing? It sounds so foolish. It sounds so weak. She's going to condemn me and feel contempt for me, and she's going to know I'm not a good meditator. How can I possibly tell her?" Finally, he worked up his courage and went to her room. He sat down and made his confession. Dipa Ma looked at him. She reached out, took his hand, and said, "That's okay. Now you can start again."

That is the love of the Buddha. Imagine for a moment the state of mind that is gentle and spacious enough to see things without harsh judgment, yet sees all things as they actually are. Within that mind-state, there is no hatred of ourselves because of our actions, speech, thoughts, desires, or fears. With the love of the Buddha, when we observe our own interior world, we don't feel ashamed, guilty, or afraid. Letting go of these impediments to clear seeing actually empowers us to be courageous and honest in viewing ourselves. Then, from understanding, compassion arises, rather than self-hatred, and we can change the course of our lives and move toward liberation.

Similarly, when we look at others, we don't feel distance or hatred; we again see clearly and with tremendous compassion. We don't remain passive or apathetic in unjust or pain-filled situations, but we are no longer driven helplessly by the force of our own judgments. With the practice of meditation, we can develop this ability to more fully love ourselves and to more consistently love others, celebrating

the love of a Buddha, which is also our own wondrous potential.

Transforming Suffering

MY TEACHER DIPA MA endured a great deal of suffering in her life, and it was this that led her to meditation
practice. Devoted to practice, she transformed her personal
grief into love for all beings. Knowing her showed me how
suffering can serve to open us to truths that might have
otherwise remained hidden, as we are forced to go through
painful experiences and find wellsprings of faith and love in
the midst of them. Dipa Ma also showed me how suffering
can serve to illuminate our connection to others.

In accordance with Indian custom, Dipa Ma entered into
an arranged marriage when she was twelve years old. At
fourteen she left her parents to join her husband in Rangoon, where he was working in the Burmese civil service.
As a young wife in a foreign country, Dipa Ma said, she
was extremely lonely and often cried. Her husband was very
gentle, however, and in time they grew closer and fell in
love. Their happiness was tested when it appeared that she
was unable to bear a child. Her husband's family even urged
him to put her aside and take another wife. Year after year
went by, but Dipa Ma did not conceive, and this was a
source of great shame and sorrow for her.

Finally, after waiting twenty years for the birth of her
first child, her infant daughter died at three months of age.
Four years later another daughter was born. The next year
Dipa Ma became pregnant again, but the son, whom she
never saw, died at birth. Mourning the deaths of her chil-

dren caused Dipa Ma's health to deteriorate severely. At the point when she was just beginning to make some peace with loss, it was discovered that she had a serious heart condition, and her doctors feared that she might die at any moment. As she faced her own frailty and the possibility of imminent death, her husband, who had been in fine health, came home one day from the office feeling ill and feverish. To her shock, he died later that day.

Dipa Ma was brokenhearted and felt as if she were actually dying of grief. She couldn't sleep, and yet she also couldn't get out of bed. She was unable to function but still had a child to raise. One day, a doctor who knew how much torment she was in said to her, "You're going to die unless you do something about the state of your mind. You should learn how to meditate."

Dipa Ma took this advice to heart and considered it carefully. She describes the moment when she asked herself, "What can I take with me when I die?" After reflection, this was her answer: "I looked around me. I looked at my dowry—my silk saris and gold jewelry—and I knew I couldn't take them with me. I looked at my daughter and knew I couldn't take her. So what could I take? I said, 'Let me go to the meditation center. Maybe I can find something there I can take with me when I die.'"

At this time Dipa Ma was still living in Burma. She found a monastery where she could practice meditation, but when she arrived, she was so weak that she had to crawl up the temple stairs in order to get into the meditation room. Yet the suffering she had endured powerfully motivated her efforts to practice. As she meditated, she looked deeply at her suffering and found great compassion for herself and for all beings. Her compassion was the expression of her healing. Through tremendous loss, Dipa Ma had come to under-

stand the fragility of life and the fact that no one is exempt
from loss and pain. Her practice brought her peace.

Dipa Ma became a revered and profound teacher, whom
I was very fortunate to study with in India. When Dipa Ma
told me that I should go back to the United States and start
teaching meditation, I was incredulous. I did not feel at all
qualified to be a meditation teacher. But she reassured me,
saying, "You really understand suffering; therefore you
should teach."

No matter whom I saw Dipa Ma interact with, she always
expressed luminous love and compassion. Her profound understanding that all of us are vulnerable to the pain of life
seemed to have removed any sense of exclusion from her
heart.

Whenever I consider my own motivation to practice, I
am awed and inspired by the image of a tiny, worn-out,
grief-stricken woman, crawling up the steps of the temple
to learn how to meditate in order to find something not
destroyed by death. Whenever I consider my personal suffering a burden, I remember Dipa Ma: how her suffering
was transformed into a path to love.

Natural Caring

ONE DAY, I had a very moving encounter on the
telephone. I had just undergone exploratory surgery to determine whether a tumor was benign or cancerous. The
woman I was speaking with, whom I knew very little, had
the kind of cancer that I had just learned I did not have. I
had only learned the results of my test a few days before,
and when I told her that the tumor had proved to be benign,

she said to me with such joy, "Sharon, I have been thinking of you so much. I am so happy for you." Her response went beyond ordinary kindheartedness. She could have said something such as, "I know how much suffering can be involved when you fear you might have cancer. I have it myself, but I am happy that you don't." This kind of comment in itself would have been a very compassionate thing to say. But her response seemed somehow even more unusual than that. In her offering of concern, she didn't take center stage; her own situation wasn't the primary reference point. In the intensity and purity of her caring, she was simply delighted that I was healthy.

What was so touching to me was the naturalness with which she did this. Amazingly, this quality of caring, without forced or contrived effort, is often expressed by people who are heroic, even those who risk their lives for strangers. When asked what made them do such a thing, they commonly reply, "What else could I do?" Though it might seem extraordinary to us, their behavior, in harmony with their worldview, is ordinary to them.

My teacher Munindra had a student, a woman named Carol, who had worked in the underground in Holland, helping Jews escape from Nazis for five years during World War II. She had been captured twice by German soldiers and tortured, and nearly all of her friends had been killed doing the same kind of work. Of herself she said only, "I was always filled with an all-consuming pity for this world, with the injustices, wars, hunger, persecutions, and cruelties suffered by the human beings living in it. I lived my life as a fighter against all I saw as wrong and especially unjust."

The rightness and naturalness of Carol's response did not mean that the work was easy or that there wasn't a price to pay. She in fact suffered recurring nightmares and deeply

ingrained fears for thirty years. But connecting and caring
were intrinsic to her vision of life, and her own integrity
compelled her to act in accordance with that vision.

We might look at Carol, or someone we know like her,
and think that we could never have the depth of caring she
exhibited. While certain conditions contributed to her actions, essentially they arose out of how she viewed life—and
it is a view possible for any of us to hold. The Eightfold
Noble Path of the Buddha, which begins with Right Understanding, or Right View, shows us how this is possible. As
the Buddha said, "Just as the dawn is the forerunner and
the first indication of the rising sun, so is Right View the
forerunner and the first indication of wholesome states."
Our view of things molds our intentions, which in turn
mold our actions. How we look at our lives becomes the
basis for how we act and how we live. When, with clear
seeing, we understand the interconnection of all of life, and
we understand that our actions do make a difference, then
we can act with uncontrived altruism.

In Pali the word for anxiety can also be translated as
"split." When we are split from our experience, when others appear as alien or separate, we feel anxious. As we close
ourselves off, or split off, we allow ourselves to be aware
of fewer feelings, and we are naturally caring toward fewer
people. We try to dispel the anxiety, to avoid it, by separat-
ing even further. Our world becomes more and more vacu-
ous and empty. Not seeing things as they really are, we can
never imagine how we could risk our lives for the sake of
others.

The practice of meditation can heal this split and bring
us back to our original connectedness. As our view of the
world is transformed, our lives are transformed. Our actions
flow from a wellspring of genuine caring, not mediated by

manipulation, self-consciousness, or anxiety. Like the gift my acquaintance on the phone offered me, this caring bestows the blessing of joy on the giver and the recipient alike. Clear vision brings forth our connection, connection gives rise to our action, and our lives become seamless expressions of how we have come to see ourselves and our world.

The Blessing of Right Effort

IN EVERY MOMENT of our existence, our potential is vast. Inherent within us is an immense possibility for awareness, courage, dedication, and love. However, many of us are conditioned to remain in a state of apparent helplessness, convinced that we cannot accomplish what we want. Our hearts shut down. We say to ourselves: "I can't do that. I am not capable of that. I'm not strong enough. I don't have the ability. . . ." In time, these beliefs about ourselves solidify into an image of who we are. And we become bound to the past, to the ways in which we may have failed, and to an inner sense of not being capable. Sadly, we basically overlook and discredit the power of our own great potential. We forget who we truly are.

This is why a correct understanding of Right Effort is so crucial. Right Effort is one part of the Buddha's Eightfold Noble Path. Traditionally, Right Effort means a courageous application of our energy toward full awareness. I've always felt that the very concept of Right Effort is a wonderful example of the profound insight contained in the Buddha's teachings. Right Effort is an acknowledgment of the conditioned suffering that is manifest in many of our thoughts about ourselves, and it is a promise that, by choosing to persevere in awareness, we can transform our lives.

Hearing the word *effort*, we may think, "Ugh, what a burden. Moment after moment, slogging through it all." But actually, Right Effort is our greatest blessing because it points to the extraordinary potential for freedom and change every one of us is capable of. My teacher Munindra said to me in a kind way, early on in my practice, "The Buddha's enlightenment solved the Buddha's problem, now you solve yours." I found that to be the most inspiring statement because it implied that I could in fact solve my own problem. The teachings of the Buddha say that no one else will accomplish our freedom from suffering for us, and that no one else needs to, because we can actually do it ourselves. It is our own effort that brings this potential to life.

Effort is the unconstrained willingness to persevere through difficulty. It is not a harsh, straining, desperate effort but, rather, an ardent and wholehearted remembrance of our capacity for freedom. Right Effort is willingness to open where we have been closed, to come close to what we have avoided, to be patient with ourselves, and to let go of our preconceptions.

When my teacher Dipa Ma first began meditating, she found that she was continually overcome by sleepiness. Talking about that time, she once said to us: "When I started doing the meditation, I was crying all the time because I wanted to follow the instructions with full regard, but I couldn't because of sleepiness. Even when standing and walking I needed to sleep. Before, I had been crying for five years and I could not sleep due to sorrow, lamentation, weakness, and other suffering. But as soon as I started meditation, all I could do was sleep."

When Dipa Ma went to her teacher to report her difficulty, he said to her, "It is a very good sign, because for the last five years you were suffering so badly you could not sleep; now you are getting sleepy. So, go mindfully. Do the meditation as instructed." Dipa Ma continued to sit, and to sleep. "But then one day," she related, "all of a sudden, I came to a state where my old sleepiness disappeared and none came to me even when I sat for some hours."

Right Effort in Dipa Ma's case meant simply not giving up. Believing in her own capacity to awaken, she was vigilant, and the fruits of her practice were extraordinary. She reports how, after this experience, she found herself saying to people, "Come to the center. You have seen how I was disheartened, because of the loss of my husband and children and my disease. But now you are finding me afresh, and I am quite happy. There is no magic. Simply by following the instructions the teachers gave, I got peace of mind. You also come, and you'll also get peace of mind."

We also can realize peace of mind. Embodying right effort to simply do the practice is a declaration of our own true potential. And our potential is boundless. When we recognize this fully, effort becomes an opportunity—rather than a burden—and a pathway that acknowledges our wholeness. "The Buddha's enlightenment solved the Buddha's problem, now you solve yours."

In the Beginning

IT IS SAID that the Buddha spoke so simply that even a seven-year-old child could understand him. Perhaps this is why it is also said that the Buddha had a fair number of fully enlightened seven-year-old disciples. I sometimes wonder what it would have been like for me as a seven-year-old to learn to meditate. In many ways it is hard to imagine, but I do think that I would have brought an openness of mind and eagerness to learn that would have stood me in good stead years later, when I finally did begin the practice.

By the time I first went to sit with Sayadaw U Pandita, I had been practicing Buddhist meditation for fourteen years. I had not yet met this Burmese meditation master, but I entered a three-month retreat under his guidance. He was a strong and demanding teacher. I often took brief notes after each period of sitting or walking meditation so that I could precisely describe my experience to him. Every day, six days a week, we saw him for private interviews.

The first time I went in for an interview, I carefully described one of my meditation periods. He looked at me and said, "Well, in the beginning it can be like that." And that was the extent of my interview! Each day I'd come in ready to describe for him an experience that I thought was wonderful or terrible or whatever, and no matter what I would report, he would say, "Well, in the beginning it can be like that." Each time he said that, I heard a voice in my head exclaiming: "Fourteen years! Fourteen years!" Silently I would retort, "I've been sitting fourteen years—I wouldn't call that being a beginner. Why are you calling me a beginner? I'm not a beginner!" It went on like that day after day: he challenging, me resentful, until one day something switched in my mind.

Many years before, when I was living in India, I had become quite lost in a model of practice that was very attainment-oriented. Despite my struggles, I thought I was doing pretty well, progressing steadily on the path to nirvana. I had gone back to the United States for a brief visit. Suzuki Roshi's book *Zen Mind, Beginner's Mind* had just come out. When I saw the book title, I thought, "Oh, I know what that book is about. It is about how, when you start practice, you have only what's called a beginner's mind. Then you practice awhile, and you accrue all of these great experiences, until one day you become supremely accomplished and you have what is called a Zen mind." I didn't buy the book; I thought I didn't need to.

Some months later, when I was back in India, somebody sent me a copy of *Zen Mind, Beginner's Mind*. When I finally read the book, I realized that I had completely misunderstood it. It was not about transcending lowly beginner's mind and one day having a sublime and extraordinary Zen mind. If anything, it was the opposite: a revelation of practice as the movement toward fully experiencing the ordinary, rather than grasping after the seemingly extraordinary. It is in ordinary mind that we find our Buddha nature, when we stop trying to have something special happen. To fully be with ordinary mind—without having expectations or making comparisons—is beginner's mind. As Suzuki Roshi described it, the spaciousness and freedom of beginner's mind is itself the attainment: "In the beginner's mind there are many possibilities; in the expert's mind there are few."

There I was, years later in this practice with U Pandita, facing exactly the same thing. One day I got it. I realized once again that it was good to be a beginner. Being a beginner means having a freshness of view and an unguarded openness to experience. It means not being burdened by ideas and concepts about what should be happening, what could be happening, what must happen next, and what I deserved to have happen. Letting go of concepts of position and status makes the practice alive in this moment, rather than stagnant. With relief, I acknowledged to myself, "I am a beginner, and I hope I continue to take joy in being a beginner."

Of course, on the very day I came to that understanding, U Pandita mysteriously stopped saying, "In the beginning it can be like that."

Reclaiming Our Power

IN THE COURSE of our lives, we too often fail to stop and recollect who we are, and the consequences are painful. As Wordsworth wrote, "Late and soon, getting and spending, we lay waste our powers." Not only in "getting and spending," but in many of our actions, our energy—our own power—is scattered and unavailable to us. A thought arises in the mind, and we end up subsumed in a cascade of associative thinking. When we emerge, we may wonder how in the world we ended up thinking longingly about Paris when the last thing we remember is thinking longingly about lunch! At times, nearly every feeling we have has the possibility of overwhelming us. We might feel delighted in one moment and stricken in the next. We run after what we think is desirable, and we pull back from what we think is undesirable. And so, lost in the past or future, swept up in judgment or worried speculation, we move onward in a state of constant reaction. Scattering an immensity of energy into all of these distractions, we sabotage our chance for equanimity and peace, and truly "lay waste our powers."

Imagine gathering all that energy back into yourself, so that it is available again for you to expend consciously— rather than having your mind scattered here and there. When we live in the present moment, we develop concentration and are reempowered. We know what we are thinking as we are thinking it, and we know what we are feeling as we are feeling it. We are not pulled into everything that arises in our minds. When the mind is concentrated, there is a sense of emotional balance. While not rejecting or cutting off feeling, this kind of concentration, known in Pali as *samattha*, brings forth an amazing steadiness and stability of mind.

In the traditional practice of concentration, we place the awareness on a single object, such as the inhalation and exhalation of the breath, or the phrases of lovingkindness, and we let go of everything else that passes through our mental and physical senses. There is almost a sense of cherishing the concentration object; sometimes, it is as if we are protecting it. But we never need to clutch it tightly or grimly; we simply practice with a quality of devotion. Devoted to the chosen object of our concentration, we stay connected to it, gently letting go of whatever distracts us from it.

Michelangelo was once asked how he would carve an elephant. He replied, "I would take a large piece of stone and take away everything that was not the elephant." Developing the force of concentration is simply seeing what is "not the elephant" and letting it go. The art of concentration is a continual letting go. We let go of that which is inessential or distracting. We let go of a thought or a feeling, not because we are afraid of it or because we can't bear to acknowledge it as a part of our experience, but because it is unnecessary. When we are practicing concentration and a thought arises in the mind—a memory, a plan, a comparison, an inviting fantasy—we let go of it. If anger arises, or self-judgment, or eager anticipation, we simply let it go, calmly returning to the object of concentration. This is what is meant by *renunciation*.

Gandhi described his life's mission in just three words:

"Renounce and enjoy." Gandhi's renunciation was a great refinement of the mind, not a terrible or bitter austerity. In the same way, throughout the practice of concentration, when we let go of distraction, our feeling tone need not be one of angry rejection. Rather, it can be an expression of our deepest motivation for freedom. We let go with the same graciousness that we might apply in offering a gift to someone. We let go as an act of generosity. Strengthening concentration, we "renounce and enjoy." We renounce that which is inessential, and relaxing into stillness, we become fully focused on the present moment.

The more we are caught in reactive movements of clinging and condemning, careening toward some thoughts and feelings and away from others, the more we suffer. Distracted from fully experiencing our lives, we "lay waste our powers." The practice of concentration is a potent method of freeing ourselves from the entanglements and limitations of this kind of instability. And so with heartfelt devotion to our deepest intention, we find ourselves letting go over and over and over again.

Happy to Concentrate

WHEN I FIRST STARTED practicing meditation, I assumed that it took a great deal of laborious, grim effort to tame the mind and develop concentration. In my first meditation retreat, I became so frustrated with the persistent wanderings of my attention that, in a frenzy, I declared to myself that the next time my attention wandered I would start to bang my head against the wall. Fortunately, the lunch bell rang just then. Standing in the lunch line, I overheard a conversation between two students I did not know. One of them was asking the other how his morning had gone. The other man replied with apparent great lightness of spirit, "I couldn't really concentrate strongly, but this afternoon may well be better."

I turned around in great shock and regarded him with disbelief. "Why isn't he as upset as I am?" I wondered. "Doesn't he take this stuff seriously at all?" This was my first meeting with Joseph Goldstein. Five and a half years later, along with Jack Kornfield and many committed friends, we would be the founders of the Insight Meditation Society. By that time, I had come to understand what lay behind Joseph's lighthearted statement.

As my practice evolved, I learned that the conditions required for concentration to develop were far from the kind of tormented struggle I had engaged in. In Buddhist psychology, every wholesome quality of mind has what is called a proximate cause. This is the condition, or the basis, that most easily and readily gives rise to a particular quality. For example, the proximate cause of *metta*, or lovingkindness, is seeing the goodness in someone, so metta most easily arises when we can see the good in someone. I had expected the proximate cause of concentration to be something like intense zeal or valiant struggle. Instead, much to my surprise, according to the Buddhist teachings the proximate cause of concentration is happiness.

As I had realized, straining to keep the mind on an object does not create the condition for concentration to most readily arise. However, when the mind is at ease, serene, and happy, we can more easily and naturally concentrate. Happiness in this sense does not mean the fleeting experience of pleasure, which inherently contains a quiet anxiety based on knowing that the moment will pass. The kind of happiness that is the proximate cause of concentration is a state of tranquillity in which our hearts are calm, open, and confident. This is the fertile ground for the growth of concentration. But how do we arrive at this state of happiness?

To some degree we arrive there by having a correct perspective—the perspective Joseph was evincing in that lunch line so many years ago. There are always what we perceive as ups and downs in practice. Meditation is a cyclical process that defies analysis, but demands acceptance. As my practice developed, I found that the ability to accept and allow for changing experience was connected to my degree of self-respect.

When my sense of self-respect was strong, I could go through difficult periods without being so disheartened. Difficulties did not reflect a lack of self-worth to me. And I could go through pleasant periods without trying to get a death-grip on them, for fear they would change and leave me feeling badly about myself. For me, self-respect definitely seemed a key component in maintaining the happiness that, in turn, helped give rise to concentration. And it became clear that my level of self-respect was rooted in how I behaved during the rest of my life, when I was not sitting on the meditation cushion. I found this truth not only in my practice, but in the classical Buddhist teachings as well.

These teachings are often presented in a causal sequence, which shows how one state of mind helps create the conditions for the arising of the next. In the *Visuddhi-magga* (The Path of Purification), a famous commentarial work of the Theravada tradition, happiness takes its place in a logical unfolding that leads from morality to ultimate liberation.

The text opens by telling us that morality is considered the foundation for the development of restraint. In Buddhism, morality does not mean a forced or puritanical abiding by rules. Morality means living with intentions that reflect our love and compassion for ourselves as well as others. As the philosopher George Santayana said, "Morality is the desire to lessen suffering in the world." When we live in harmony with the innate truth of our interdependence, we want to refrain from doing harmful acts. This leads to the next mental condition of restraint.

Restraint is the foundation for the development of the absence of remorse. When we restrain a momentary impulse to do a harmful act, we are able to see the impermanence and transparency of the desire that initially arose. Having avoided harmful action, we also avoid the guilt, fear of discovery, and the confusion and regret that come when we forget that what we do has consequences.

The positive condition that results from restraint is called "gladdening." Absence of remorse is the foundation for the development of gladdening. Gladdening is the state of lightness and ease we find in our lives as we increasingly care for ourselves and other beings. Because we genuinely experience a connection to others, we let go of actions that are hurtful and do fewer things that keep us feeling separate from others. Thus our common, dispiriting sense of loneliness and alienation is relieved. Gladdening is the foundation for the development of happiness.

In this way we arrive at happiness—the happiness of peace, composure, and strength. This is happiness that is not going to fracture as conditions change, as people behave in disappointing ways, as we do not get what we want. This is happiness based on knowing our interconnectedness, on the integrity of acting from our deepest values. It is based on a mind at ease. This is self-respect.

It then follows, according to the *Visuddhi-magga*, that happiness is the foundation for the development of tranquillity. Rather than the turbulence and agitation that we experience when the mind is full of worry, remorse, and guilt, the mind is quieter. Because there is not a great bundle of complexity that we need to disentangle and make amends for, we can be more peaceful in this moment. Tranquillity, arising from happiness, is the foundation for the development of concentration. (It was obviously this tranquillity that I was lacking in that retreat long ago.)

Concentration is steadiness of mind, the feeling we have when we are one-pointed and powerful in our attention. When we can concentrate, a door opens to insight and wisdom. Concentration is thus the foundation for the development of correct knowledge and vision. This means being able to see things as they actually are, without so quickly distorting the experience through the filter of our hopes and fears. It is the release from these filters that leads us personally, intimately, to trust in our own sense of truth. Correct knowledge and vision, once firmly a part of our lives, is the foundation for the development of dispassion.

Dispassion does not mean coldness or indifference but, rather, a spaciousness of mind in which we enjoy a sense of wholeness and sufficiency no matter what the particular transitory life situation. It is equanimity in the face of the changing circumstances we continually meet. Whether we get what we want or not, we can see things in perspective. We can do what needs to be done to try to alleviate our own or others' suffering, and we can do it from a place of inner peace. This was Joseph in the lunch line, though at the time I thought he was frivolous for not torturing himself, as I was doing myself.

Dispassion is the foundation for the development of the fading away of greed and anger. Once we are moving through life's circumstances with more balance and the happiness of self-respect, we are not so mechanically driven by old habits of reaction, like desperately trying to hold on to pleasure or flee from pain. These old habits cannot take root in our hearts in quite the same way. Even when they arise, there is a porous quality to them, so that we need not be afraid of them any longer, and we can choose not to follow their call.

The fading away of greed and hatred is the foundation for liberation. Liberation is "the sure heart's release"—an understanding of the truth so powerful that there is no turning back from it. When we are not approaching our experience with an agenda, trying to have it complete a sense of lack in ourselves, we can pay careful attention to what is arising. We can open to life and learn from it, for our own experience reveals the truth of all of life. When we can pay careful, unbiased attention, we discover the cause of our suffering as well as our freedom from suffering.

This sequence, as described by the *Visuddhi-magga*—morality, restraint, gladdening, happiness, tranquillity, concentration, dispassion, the fading away of greed and anger, liberation—is as natural as the movement of the wind. When happiness is seen in the context of this process, it becomes an integral part of our spiritual life. We dedicate our intentions to nonharming, to love and compassion, and we are led to the prospect of freedom.

While happiness is an end in itself, one of the fruits of meditation, it is also the state of mind we can have right now, simply by respecting ourselves and living a life of caring. This is the happiness that is an essential ingredient for the ultimate liberation of our minds from suffering.

The Awareness of Breath

IT IS SAID that as a child, the Buddha spontaneously practiced mindfulness of breathing, and on the eve of his enlightenment he remembered this practice as he searched for perfect balance of mind. *Anapana*, the Pali word for awareness of the breath as it enters and leaves the nostrils, is one of the most fundamental objects of concentration that the Buddha taught.

When I went to India in 1970, I went specifically to learn how to meditate. By January of 1971, I entered my first intensive retreat. I had no experience at all in meditation, but I did have many ideas about what esoteric, complex practice I would learn. The first meditation instruction I was ever given was to be aware of my breath. The simplicity was shocking.

Anapana is a fundamental practice for a number of reasons. The breath is natural and uncontrived. When I first began practicing, I would become anxious about the next breath, as though I had to create it. But if I said to myself, "You're breathing anyway, you might as well just be aware of it," I could relax. Being aware of the natural breath, we bring forth ease of mind and body.

The breath is happening right now, in this moment. As we pay attention to the breath, we might find that our attention wanders to the past, comparing the breath that is happening in the present to one that has gone before. Or attention might wander to the future, anticipating when we must stand up and eat breakfast and go to work, all while the current breath is still happening.

One of the most powerful insights of my early practice came about when I saw how often I was "leaning forward" looking for the next breath. I realized that I could simply settle back into the present. It felt startlingly balanced and completely right, as though I were returning to a natural home that I had been unknowingly missing. With this kind of mindfulness, we notice both the tendency to fall back into the past and lean forward into the future, and then we can relax and be in balance. In this way, we feel the difference between being scattered and experiencing the wholeness of our full presence.

Awareness of the breath serves as a clear mirror, not for or against anything, but simply reflecting the moment, without the obstruction of concepts and judgments. We can freely let pass whatever arises in the mind, as we maintain attention on the breath. Perhaps we have a tendency to judge: "My breath isn't good enough, deep enough, broad enough, subtle enough, clear enough." I certainly did, as I found the simple act of breathing fraught with projected meaning about what a deficient person I was. Returning to the breath, as we continually let go of these judgments, we give birth to compassion for ourselves.

In this practice of anapana, each breath, from the beginning through the middle to the end, becomes our universe. Feeling the breath as it enters and leaves the nostrils—rather than watching it as if we were distant observers—we become one with the breath, connected with its changing sensations. As I felt the breath, my tendencies to remove myself from the moment and to pull back were challenged, and I found an intimacy with my own life.

In being mindful of our breathing, we see clearly the fragility of life, as we are completely dependent on every intake of air. As we experience the constantly changing sensations that arise and pass away, we begin to watch the solidity of the body dissolve, bringing forth understanding of the nature of change. For life itself is turning on each breath. One of my teachers once said to me, "You know, life depends on your breathing in again once you've breathed out."

The essence of anapana practice—as of all meditation practices—is the ability to begin again. We may be lost in the past, lost in the future, or lost in judgment, but once we realize we have been distracted, right in that moment we can begin again and reconnect with the breath. While it might be tempting to spend some time elaborating on our distraction or judging ourselves for having not been with the breath, by letting go and just beginning again, we are at once experiencing a totality of connection and an immediacy of awareness. In the beginning of my practice, I often lost touch with the breath. When I emerged from my fantasy, I would at times spend the rest of the sitting period chastising myself for having become lost: "Why did you do that? Yesterday you didn't do that quite so much. No one else is getting distracted, only you."

The irony of that experience was that the original fantasy might have distracted me for five minutes, while my getting lost in judgment distracted me for a further twenty minutes and caused even more suffering. As we practice in this way—seeing that no matter what outrageous, difficult, seductive, or foolish thought has arisen, we can begin again—a deep trust in ourselves takes shape.

By beginning again, we become present. The Pali word *bhavana*, usually translated as "meditation," literally means "causing something to become," "calling into existence," or "bringing forth." It conveys a sense of giving birth. As we practice mindfulness of breath meditation, we are bringing forth ease, presence, intimacy, compassion, wisdom, and trust. Simply by being with our breath, we are giving birth to our wholeness.

The Heavenly Abodes

I TRAVEL TO MANY PLACES in the world to teach the practice of the four *brahma-viharas*, or "Heavenly Abodes"—lovingkindness, compassion, sympathetic joy, and equanimity. I am continually surprised that, no matter where I go, so many people consider these states of mind as weaknesses. Students at a retreat will say, "If I am loving and compassionate, I will allow myself to be abused and hurt." "To me those are just sweet sentiments, but it's not really possible to live like that." Sadly, this attitude misses what tremendous strength lies in the Brahma Viharas. They are the source of acknowledging and cultivating our profound connection with life.

The writer Wendell Berry says that "the smallest unit of health is a community." Community is another way of saying connection, and connection is life itself. This is revealed again and again in various studies. For instance, people who have suffered a heart attack seem to heal more quickly if they have pets, as compared with those who do not. When all other variables are controlled, cancer patients who join a support group tend to live longer than those who do not. Those who are prayed for when sick, even if they are unaware of the prayers, do better than those who are not prayed for. The mysterious root of healing is connection.

The four Brahma Viharas are practices that inspire and deepen our connection to each other. In this way, they extend healing not only to others but also to ourselves. The word *healing* shares the same root meaning as "wholeness." We do not exist as separate, isolated beings; we are part of a community of all beings. That is our wholeness. The Brahma Viharas are practices that cultivate our faith in our own loving hearts and in the strength of our connection with others.

The first Brahma Vihara, lovingkindness, is the practice of friendship. We may believe that we are not capable of loving ourselves, let alone all of the beings in the world. Steadfastly practicing lovingkindness invokes the capacity to love that is inviolate within us. As we wish love, peace, and happiness for ourselves and others, we learn to include all beings and all aspects of all beings, including ourselves, in our hearts.

When I first practiced lovingkindness intensively, probably the most amazing moment came when I recognized that, indeed, I was capable of this much love. I actually sat there dazed, thinking, "Is this me?" In fact, we all are capable of tremendous love, but until we untangle our conditioning, our capacity for connection remains hidden or distorted.

Dipa Ma, who so embodied lovingkindness, once went to Sylvia Boorstein's house to lead a class. Sylvia had a large dog, a breed called Akita, that was quite formidable looking. Normally guests hesitated on the threshold, waiting for solid reassurance that the dog was harmless. However, when Dipa Ma saw the dog, she just sailed right in. The dog rose up to greet her, putting his paws on Dipa Ma's shoulders. Dipa Ma was a tiny woman, well under five feet tall, so they were just about of equal size. Dipa Ma put her hands on the dog's head and blessed him! No one seemed excluded from Dipa Ma's offering of blessings or from her sense of community.

The next Brahma Vihara is compassion, literally meaning the quivering of our heart in response to pain or suffering. Our own pain and the pain of others can become vehicles for a deeply moving connection. Oftentimes, when we are in pain ourselves, we can be filled with resentment, wondering why we should have such suffering. Or we may feel very isolated, perhaps obsessively blaming ourselves for something we said or did, or something we didn't say or do, that we consider to be the cause of the pain. And we may be averse to seeing suffering in others because we find it unbearable or distasteful, or we find it threatening to our own happiness. All of these various reactions to the suffering in the world make us want to turn away from life.

Conversely, compassion manifests in us as the offering of solidarity rather than withdrawal. Because compassion is a state of mind that is itself open, abundant, and inclusive, it allows us to meet pain more directly. With direct seeing, we know that we are not alone in our suffering, and that no one need feel alone when in pain. Seeing our oneness is the beginning of our compassion, and it allows us to reach beyond aversion and separation to the understanding that our community is everyone.

Sympathetic joy, the third Brahma Vihara, is the practice of actively taking delight in the happiness of others, rather than feeling threatened or diminished, as if the happiness of another takes something away from us. When I began to practice this way of seeing, I found that my normal conditioned reaction was to feel as though there was a limited amount of happiness in the world, and the more someone else had, the less there was going to be left for me. But, in reality, with strong sympathetic joy, we are able to feel happy when others are happy; we rejoice and take delight in their happiness.

As the Dalai Lama expresses it, there are so many other people in this world, it simply makes sense to make their happiness as important as our own, because then our chances of delight "are enhanced six billion to one." Those are very good odds. When the happiness of others is our own happiness, we are acknowledging our connection to each other. We become part of a community.

The fourth Brahma Vihara is equanimity, which in some ways feels very different from the other three. This is because the predominant tone of equanimity is one of calm. In this spacious stillness of mind, we can be connected to whatever is happening around us, connected to others, but without our habitual reactions of careening toward what is pleasant and pulling away from what is unpleasant. This, in effect, allows the other Brahma Viharas to grow boundlessly.

Without equanimity, we would offer friendship only as long as our offering is acknowledged and appreciated, or as long as someone responds in kind. We would offer compassion to ourselves only when we weren't overcome by our pain, and compassion to others only when we weren't overcome by their suffering. We would offer sympathetic joy only when we did not feel threatened or envious. When we cultivate equanimity, our tremendous capacity to connect can blossom, for we do not have to push away or cling to anything that may happen.

Sometimes in learning meditation the instruction is, "Sit like a mountain. Sit with a sense of strength and dignity. Be steadfast, be majestic, be natural and at ease in awareness. No matter how many winds are blowing, no matter how many clouds are swirling, no matter how many lions are prowling, be intimate with everything and sit like a mountain." This is an image of equanimity. We feel everything, without exception, and we relate to it through our own strength of awareness, not through habitual reactions. Like when Dipa Ma blessed the "fierce" Akita, we find the freedom to connect to everyone.

All four of these practices are accomplished by inclining the mind toward love and connection. We begin with someone for whom it is easy for us to feel lovingkindness or compassion or sympathetic joy or equanimity. Slowly the field of our attention expands to include others we care for, those to whom we feel indifferent, those we dislike, and finally all beings everywhere.

In doing these practices, we are not striving for artificial sentiments nor attempting to conform to an abstract idea of a spiritual person. We are not squashing feelings of outrage that we might have, or repressing our healthy-minded fear. Love, compassion, sympathetic joy, and equanimity do not distort our ability to see clearly, but rather, as we realize that we are together with all beings, they transform the reasons we work to create change. Our motivation, or our mental posture, becomes one of inclusion rather than separation. And as we grow stronger in the practice of the Brahma Viharas, we find that we can honestly and directly look at problems, and take strong action as we take care of ourselves and others. We find the ultimate healing truth of connection.

Just the Way It Is

ONE AUTUMN a friend of mine called me after returning from several months of meditation practice in Thailand. When I asked how he was, he answered, "I'm doing very well. I'm just hanging up my skeleton." I was a little bewildered but, given the season, I ventured, "Oh, for Halloween?"

"No," he said. "I just spent a month of intensive meditation contemplating skeletons, and I was really absorbed in it." I asked, "Well, how was that for you?"

"At first, it was absolutely disgusting," he replied. "But over time, a special kind of clarity came—one of no pretense, no social niceties. I'd walk into the dining room and see myself as a skeleton and everyone else as a skeleton. It is just the way it is."

As he spoke, I thought of an exhibit in the Folk Art Museum in Santa Fe where miniature figures of people are engaged in many common activities—such as cooking and playing music—but everybody in the exhibit is a skeleton; so skeletons are playing the violin, frying eggs, and so forth. It is definitely suggestive of a hidden reality that we don't normally want to consider!

Buddhist practices like the one my friend had done are part of what are called *asubha* meditations, traditionally translated as "contemplating the loathsome nature of the body." While it would seem that such practices might give rise to fear and repulsion, they are not meant to provoke these responses at all, but rather to bring freedom and clarity to the mind.

This result may seem unlikely. A more accurate translation of the Pali word *asubha* can make the potential fruit of this kind of practice easier to understand. *Asubha* actually means "that which goes against the current." And these practices certainly go against the current in our society! They go against the current of regarding our bodies as objects we must beautify without limit to meet certain cultural standards. They go against the current of believing our bodies can remain young and healthy indefinitely, and believing we can rely on our bodies not to let us down.

In a society like ours, it goes against the current to look straight at the true nature of the body. It is constantly suggested to us—through advertising, media, movies—that it is humiliating to have a body that is not perfect, that is not perfectly functioning. Given how truly out of control the body is, this kind of social conditioning creates a great deal of heartache and fruitless self-judgment. To be sure, we affect our bodies by our habits and the quality of our lives, but we cannot absolutely control the body; we cannot keep it from changing. And there is no one among us, regardless of how much money we spend in pursuit of attractiveness, who will not die. Yet, death is kept hidden, almost as if it were unnatural and disgraceful, as if somebody has done something wrong when they die. We are freed from so much suffering when we recognize that, as the poet William Butler Yeats said, we are "fastened to a dying animal."

Asubha meditation practices are all about coming to realize the body for what it truly is, and this is greatly liberating. This has nothing to do with not loving ourselves or not cherishing our lives. It has nothing to do with that deep, cold place within us that is afraid that we are ultimately not lovable. It has to do with having the courage to open to what is usually hidden. We simply look and see what is actually the nature of things. When we see the truth, there's nothing to be afraid of or repulsed by. The nature of the body is something we all share.

When we live conscious of the truth, we are free of the constraints of pretense and denial. After all, we live in a society where corpses are made up as if going to a party; where people too often die alone, without support; where unpleasantness of all kinds is sanitized and taken away by somebody else, so that we don't have to look at it. No wonder we are so often tired and afraid. Trying to avoid looking at the natural flow of life is fearful, tiring work. And it creates suffering not only for ourselves, but for others, as we collude in the great myth of the body's unchanging nature.

Disease, decay, blood, guts, and skeletons are disturbing images, but thinking about them puts a lot of things in perspective. How ironic that our recognition of the component parts of the body is liberating. So if at times we realize that the person frying our eggs is a skeleton, and we who will be eating them are also skeletons, perhaps that can free us to hold everything in perspective, to not hate our bodies as they age, to not reject those who are sick or dying, to not resent things being the way that they are. As my friend said when his meditation led him to see everyone as a skeleton, "It is just the way it is."

Returning Home

I ONCE WENT FOR A WALK with a friend in Mount Auburn Cemetery in Cambridge, Massachusetts. She and I wandered around, engrossed in talking about our experiences of living in India many years ago. As we were walking, it grew darker, and all of a sudden we realized that we were lost. We were so lost that I thought we were going to end up spending the night in the cemetery. We walked and walked in the deepening dusk until it was quite dark. I felt terrible uncertainty as we walked through the enormous maze, trying to find our bearings. You can imagine how similar every tombstone looked in the dark. We would say to one another, "Did we pass the Carters already? How long ago? Which way were we going when we walked by their mausoleum?" Finally, after hours of searching, we found the gate, locked long before. After another interminable wait, the guard appeared, and we were free.

That experience of being completely lost is a good analogy for the mind-state of delusion. In delusion we have no
idea where we are or where we are going. When delusion is
strong in the mind, we feel as I did walking through that
dark cemetery—filled with uncertainty, even dread—and
we begin to get more and more agitated. "What will happen
to me if I take a step to the left? What will happen to me if
I take two steps to the right? What's next? And what's after
that?"

In Pali, the word for delusion is *moha*, which means to be
stupefied. In this state we feel bewildered and helpless. The
mind is dull, confused, and restless. In the state of delusion,
we feel unsettled in our own minds, our own beings, as if
we don't belong there, as if we are inhabiting some strange
place. Life takes on the quality of being a puzzling array of
pieces that don't seem to fit together. We can't quite see
where things are connected, how they are related, how they
are joined. Failing to see things as they actually are, we feel
cut loose from a sense of connection to anything. But when
we get even a glimpse of those connections, we are moved
to let go of delusion and develop wisdom. Wise attention,
or mindfulness, transforms delusion into wisdom. Being
mindful allows us to see things according to their true nature. Wise attention means connecting to our experience
without reacting according to habit. This quality melts our
confusion and allows us to discover our own integrity and
the interrelatedness of all of life. No matter what is happening, we can approach our situation with clarity and calm.

Had my friend and I been able to find peace in ourselves,
we could have been peaceful even in the cemetery. The
Thai monk Ajahn Chah likens delusion to being without a
home. He said, "When we have no real home, we are like
aimless travelers, out on the road, going this way for a

while, then that way. Until we return to our real home, we feel ill at ease whatever we are doing." Many of us come to meditation practice specifically to find our real home.

After wandering this way and that, when we find our home it is like turning on the light in a dark room. It doesn't matter if the room has been dark for a day or a week or ten thousand years. When we turn on the light of wise attention, we can see clearly. Seeing clearly, we realize that we have no distance to travel in any direction to find our real home, where we belong, where we can be at ease—it is right where we are.

The Heart of Practice

THE FIRST RETREATS we had for families at the Insight Meditation Society were specifically designed for parents of our students. Introducing them to the practice was a way to dispel their concerns about their children's strange new hobby. One student, apprehensive about her mother coming to learn how to meditate, said, "My mother is the kind of woman who would say 'The goddamn birds kept me up all night.' " In fact, her mother said exactly that after her first night here! But by the end of the week, she was listening in a whole different way. She had begun to simply hear, letting go of the judgments that might attach themselves to sounds like birds in the middle of the night.

There are so many ways to hear a sound. We might hear a certain noise and become reactive and upset, finding it unpleasant. If we think the sound is a pleasant one, we might want it to go on and on. If the sound strikes us as neither pleasant nor unpleasant, however, we may only "half hear" it. Or, we can hear a sound directly, without judgment or conceptual elaboration—simply as a sensory event—and the whole world can open up before us. To experience the phenomena of the world in this direct way is the essence of mindfulness.

Mindfulness is a quality of awareness that sees directly whatever is happening in our experience and meets it face to face, without the intrusion of bias, without adding such forces as grasping, aversion, or delusion to the experience. Conditioned to live in a state of grasping, we make futile attempts to keep pleasant experiences going on forever. Conditioned to live in anger and fear, we recoil from painful experiences as though we could prevent them from happening. Conditioned to live in delusion, we "space out" and become disconnected from the moment when an experience is not strikingly pleasant or unpleasant.

If we add together all of the times when we do not experience life fully because desire and attachment keep us from being present; and all the times that we try to separate from what is, out of anger or fear; and all of the times that we are spaced out, we end up with a pretty big pile of moments. What is left over is a tiny parcel of mindful moments when we are fully alive, not lost in clinging, resisting, or disconnecting. This is a shockingly limited way to live.

It is possible to be awake and present with balance, serenity, and understanding, whether our experience is pleasant, unpleasant, or neutral. This is the power of mindfulness. Mindfulness is a penetrative and profound awareness characterized by nonsuperficiality. Traditionally, the quality of mindfulness is illustrated by comparing what happens if you throw a cork into water versus what happens when you throw a rock. Superficial awareness is like the cork that floats on top of the water. The rock, in contrast, sinks right to the bottom.

Another way of understanding this quality of awareness is to consider what happens if we pour water into a cup. The water doesn't stay in one place—it fills whatever space there is. In the same way, mindfulness suffuses the object of attention, spreading over it entirely. When we are mindful, we suffuse our experience with awareness. When we hear a sound, our awareness moves deeply into the moment of hearing.

When we are mindful, when we can meet what is happening directly, then there is great vitality in our world. Rather than seeing through the filters of our conditioned hopes and fears, we can be with things as they are. When we are mindful, we look with meditative vision, or as the Sufis say, with "eyes unclouded by longing."

Seeing in this way might be likened to what happens when we get to know someone new. When we first meet a person, we might want them to be a certain way, and we might be careless in our observations so that we create a fabrication of who they are based on their surface appearance. Slowly, as our projections lessen, we pay more attention and can see through the elements of the facade. We come closer and closer to the actual, living reality of that person. In the same way, when we are being mindful, we come closer to the actual living reality of our experience.

Mindfulness can go anywhere. It is not limited to any particular experience. You might say, as did our student's mother, "Well, I couldn't be mindful because it was too noisy." But that would be a misperception of mindfulness. We can be mindful of quiet, and we can be mindful of noise. We can be mindful of tremendously resenting the noise.

We can be mindful of everything in our experience. Mindfulness is an infinitely inclusive quality of mind.

It is said that awareness does not take the shape of its object, which means that we can be mindful of pleasure in one moment, of sadness in the next moment, and then of boredom, and the nature of mindfulness does not alter. Whatever we are being aware of, the nature of the awareness itself is spacious, open, and free.

Practicing mindfulness is like taking a journey or unraveling a great mystery. There are countless times every day when we lose mindfulness and become lost in reaction or disconnected from what is happening. But as soon as we recognize that we have lost it, we can begin again. In fact, the moment we recognize that we have lost mindfulness, we have already regained it, because the recognition is itself a function of awareness.

When we are willing to continually begin again, the power of mindfulness reveals itself. The practice reaches fruition in each arising moment as well as in future moments. Mindfulness is not something abstract or far away; it comes alive for each of us the moment we begin, and as we begin again. This is the very heart of the practice.

Drop by Drop

DURING A MEDITATION RETREAT, students often come to interviews ashamed and upset because they have had a hard time staying mindful, as though they had slid down a mountain and were wondering if they could ever crawl back up again. Sometimes it seems as if they are not sure they even deserve to try, having strayed so far from the path. But there is no distance at all to traverse to becoming mindful again, or loving, or compassionate. We need simply to recognize that these qualities are already right at hand, in each moment of awareness.

In my own practice, one of the simple images the Buddha used has been hugely helpful. The Buddha said, "The mind will get filled with qualities like mindfulness, like loving-kindness, moment by moment—just the way a bucket gets filled with water drop by drop." As soon as I heard that image, I clearly saw two powerful tendencies in my mind: One was to stand beside the bucket, lost in fantasy about how utterly exciting and wonderful it would be when the bucket was filled. Meanwhile, as I was lost in the glories of my some-day enlightenment, I was neglecting to add the next drop. The other tendency, equally strong, was to stand by the bucket in despair over how empty it was and how much more there was to go—once again not having the patience, humility, and good sense to add one drop right in that moment by being mindful.

We may not only be lost in judgment about our own buckets, but also have a tendency to spend a lot of time peering over into other people's buckets to see how well they are doing. Is theirs fuller than ours? Is it emptier? What's going on over there? Actually, this process of comparison is misleading and irrelevant. First of all, what we see from the outside is our projection of someone's apparent experience. In fact, "the bucket" doesn't get filled by the accumulation of special experiences anyway; it gets filled by moments of mindfulness or moments of lovingkindness. What is essential is not what happens to someone, but how they relate to what happens to them. Comparing experiences has nothing to do with perceiving anyone's depth of spiritual understanding or their compassion or awareness.

Comparing ourselves to others, or even to our own ideas of progress, leads us to objectify qualities such as mindfulness and lovingkindness, making them into something to be attained and held on to in order to make us into good people. When we objectify people or states of mind, we relate to them in terms of whether we have them or don't have them. Inevitably, distance or separation is created between self and some "thing," or between self and other. Once there is separation, there is fear of loss, and we are once again in the cycle of clinging and anxiety.

Mindfulness and lovingkindness are not objects we can either have or not have. We can never lose them. We may lose touch with these qualities of heart, but right here and now we can recover them. There is no remedial work to be done nor any struggle necessary to try to regain them. In every single moment, regardless of what is happening, we can be mindful and compassionate. In an instant, the mind can turn and retouch these qualities to know them again. The process is one of recognizing that full awareness can be found in any moment. In this sense the bucket is completely full with every drop.

The Object of Our Desire

A FRIEND OF MINE spent many years in a monastery in Korea, practicing with one of the most famous Zen masters of our time. At one point, she brought him to the United States. The one place he wanted to go to more than any other was Las Vegas. When she told me that story, I was shocked. "He didn't gamble, did he?" I asked. "Oh no," my friend said. "Many Koreans who had visited the United

States had gone back and talked to him about all of the bright lights in Las Vegas. He wanted to go to see all the bright lights." The Zen master in Las Vegas was certainly having a very different perception of the scene than most tourists there. For most, the lights are alluring for what they promise. I could imagine the Zen master walking along with the crowd, unattracted to the promise but greatly delighting in the lights themselves.

Our world is rather like the main street in Las Vegas: glittering with enticing pleasures that we reach out for because of the happiness each one promises. But in order to develop a relationship to those "bright lights" that will bring us true happiness, we need to learn how to enjoy the display without becoming attached to it. The spiritual path, after all, is about happiness—tremendous happiness—but one that is not tied up with infatuation or confusion, and one that is not subject to constant change.

We all like pleasant experiences and are fortunate to enjoy them, but if we become lost in attachment, that enjoyment inevitably turns to clinging and then we suffer. At a Buddhist-Christian conference I attended at Gethsemani Monastery in Kentucky, His Holiness the Dalai Lama was speaking about the tour of the monastery he had been given earlier that day. He began by saying that he was quite impressed that the monastery was able to support itself through the manufacture of cheeses and fruitcakes. Then, in the midst of this formal presentation, with television cameras rolling, the Dalai Lama said, "I was presented with a piece of the homemade cheese, which was very good, but really I wanted some cake!" He laughed uproariously and repeated, "It was so unfortunate—really I was hoping someone would offer me some cake, but no one did!" His childlike candor was wonderful, with nothing manipulative about

it. Clearly, he could be quite happy without a piece of fruitcake, and some part of his state of happiness was the very
ability to laugh at his desire for cake, as well as being able
to speak about it unabashedly before dignitaries of two reli-
gions and a television audience!

It is wonderful to get what we want, and we are fortunate
when the fruitcake is offered and we can enjoy it. But when
we want something out of an effort to fill an aching desire
within, looking for some sense of completion, then we are
lost in attachment. We are trying to fill an emptiness that
no object can ever fill. Something such as pure awareness
or deep compassion might fill it, but not any ephemeral
object.

The message that we often receive from our society is
that our lives are lacking. We do not have enough, we ourselves are lacking in some way, and if only we would buy
this one thing, then finally we might be happy. We very
much want to find a stable, undeviating, secure happiness
simply by obtaining something (for obtaining a thing is
something we can sometimes do). Likewise, we hope that
we can then keep what we have obtained from ever changing (which is something we can never do). Reaching out
time and time again, we fixate on the person, thing, or experience that we desire, and attempt to claim it as "ours,"
trying to control it and keep it from going away.

One of the amazing things about the mind is that it can
become attached to anything. We can be attached to a feeling of calm, or we can be attached to intensity. We can be
attached to crisis, catharsis, stupor—to anything. We think
that we desperately need whatever is the object of our attachment in order to feel alive, to feel complete.

The tremendous irony of attachment is that we become
lost in this state of mind precisely because we want to feel

connected rather than separate and isolated. We mistakenly believe that holding on will reinforce connection, renewing and deepening it. Yet life itself is change. We may struggle in defiance against this fundamental truth of impermanence. We may repair or remove or replace "objects" as we try to sustain happiness, or try to convince ourselves that we are connected as we reach out to the next passing thing, but the happiness of true connection will remain out of reach.

Attachment is taught as the first of the five hindrances that commonly arise in the mind, making concentration difficult and luring us away from mindfulness and into unconscious actions that ultimately cause us pain. The other four hindrances are traditionally known as aversion, sloth and torpor, restlessness, and doubt. The hindrances are the expression of our seeming separateness. When we misunderstand these mind-states and compulsively follow them, they bring us suffering. However, when we work skillfully with them, including them in our field of awareness and compassion, they can actually provide rich ground for discovering our inherent connection to all of life.

How do we work skillfully with attachment? Our tendency is to focus so strongly on the object of our attachments that we disregard the feeling of attachment itself. The "bright lights" are so distracting, so entrancing, that we get drawn in without noticing the tone of the attachment that we are experiencing. When we directly experience the feeling of attachment, we stop being so infatuated with it, and we break the trance. When we can feel the pain of attachment in its naked form, we stop allowing it to rule our lives and diminish our capacity for enjoyment and connection.

Regarding attachment with mindfulness gives us tremendous courage. We not only enjoy the times we get what we want but also are not swept away by disappointment when we don't. Mindfulness gives us immense spaciousness of mind. We can relax from our habit of clinging, of reifying experience, of contracting our minds around what we want. It also gives us the ability to feel compassion, as we see the pain we and others are led into over and over again by the hindrance of attachment. Finally, we find that we do not have to hold on to something, or always get what we want in order to be happy. We realize that courage, spaciousness of mind, and compassion are themselves the ingredients of lasting happiness.

Anger

ONE DAY SOMEONE sent me a note by e-mail asking about the nature of anger. I replied by saying, "Well, one of the painful things about anger is the tendency we have when we're angry to put people in a box." We bind the object of our anger, whether ourselves or another, to a certain definition and cannot see beyond it. Just after sending the reply, something went very wrong in the relationship between my computer and my printer. Terribly frustrated, I got down on my hands and knees and started unplugging cords from one place and plugging them into another, trying to fix the problem. The most computer-literate person on our staff at the Insight Meditation Society (IMS), where I live, had gone away on vacation, and I found myself feeling angry at him. My mind was so filled with thinking "Why isn't he here when I need him?" that I completely overlooked the fact that I had strongly urged him to go away, to take a break from IMS, and had in fact helped to arrange the trip. I was also angry at myself for not being more knowledgeable about computers, chiding myself, "Why can't you be the kind of person who can fix these things?" In the meantime, despite my self-image, I managed to solve the problem.

Soon after, I got back on-line, and there was my correspondent again, this time saying, "I don't know exactly what you mean by saying that anger leads to our putting people in boxes." I immediately wrote back to him describing how I had just done exactly that to my computer-literate friend as well as to myself.

Anger is the mind-state that dislikes what is happening and strikes out against it. Anger wants to create distance and disconnection. It is a state of mind that does not cling to things but rather, searching for faults, pushes away from them. Think about what happens when you feel angry: The mind gets very narrow and tight. It isolates "the problem" and fixates solely on someone or something. Lost in this state, we get tunnel vision and see no way out. We forget the law of change. And so we put people, ourselves, and situations in boxes: "This is how it is, and this is how it's always going to be." Because we don't see many alternatives and can't imagine anything beyond our injuries or deficits, we feel overwhelmed and we panic. We lose perspective and forget that things do change.

Lost in anger, we tend to think we should be able to control the events of our lives. We blame ourselves when we can't, even when these events are completely outside of anyone's control. I did not make the computer and printer stop connecting properly, but I was so angry with myself for my imagined inability to fix it, that I scarcely noticed I was, in fact, fixing it.

When anger is a strong factor of mind, it is often a conse-
quence of projecting outward our inner dissatisfaction.
Everywhere we look, we see what is wrong. When we walk
into a room, we are bound to see what we don't like. We
don't like what that person is wearing, we don't like who
that person is with, we don't like the wallpaper, and on and
on. We all probably know someone who never seems satis-
fied in any situation, who has a perpetually soured expression on their face, who is often just simply reactive—all this
from the sheer habitual force of being angry.

Anger, in itself, is not best viewed as bad or wrong. It
is simply another state of mind that arises in reaction to
circumstances. It is natural to feel angry at times, especially
when confronted by cruelty or injustice, and this anger can
burn through the fog of apathy that surrounds such issues.
When we find ourselves in a situation where we feel ignored
or unrecognized, where others have put us in a box, we
again might well react with anger. Even though this is un-
derstandable, it is still painfully limiting and confusing. Our
minds become narrow and our hearts shut off. We feel very
alone, and we may seek to gain control without perhaps
fully understanding a situation.

We need to understand how anger functions and how it
affects us, not condemn ourselves for feeling it. Does anger
give us the energy to make change in a sustained way? Does
it allow us to see clearly? Does it actually enable us to control a situation, a person, our body, or our mind? Does it
give us skill in making change? Or, when we're angry, do
we lash out in ways that prevent effective change?

It's important to investigate the nature of anger because
it is such a powerful energy and can be so destructive. When
we can face our anger without being afraid of it, or angry
about it, or defenseless in the face of it, then we can come

close to it. When we are able to look closely at anger, we see the threads of different feelings—the sadness and the fear woven throughout it—and we can see its true nature. When we can uncover the helplessness and powerlessness that often feed anger, we transform them. In being mindful of these feelings, we actually use the sheer energy of anger—without getting lost in it or overcome by its tremendously deluding and fixating quality—to reveal instead the courage and compassion that have been concealed.

Waiting to Live

WHEN I PRACTICED MEDITATION in Burma, we had to keep the traditional eight Buddhist precepts, which include not eating solid food after noon. In fact, with lunch served at ten o'clock in the morning, all eating is over by 10:30 A.M. After that there's no tea, no food, no edible distraction whatsoever. I remember the long walk from the dining room back to my room, knowing that there was going to be nothing else to eat for the rest of the entire day. What awaited me, in all those hours between 10:30 in the morning and 11:00 at night, was intensive meditation practice: just sitting and walking, sitting and walking, sitting and walking. With every step back from that dining room in the midmorning light, I would somehow get more and more tired. By the time I'd get to my room, I'd be seriously sleepy. It wasn't that I actually needed sleep, but rather, the prospect of anticipated lack of stimulation was so frightening that I just wanted to lie down and forget everything.

In our lives, we get used to a certain degree of stimulation. In fact, we rely on it to keep us awake, to help us feel alive. In meditation practice, as we become increasingly sensitive to subtlety, we discover how much we are "experience junkies," craving ever-increasing levels of stimulation. As we practice meditation, we get used to stillness and eventually are able to make friends with the quietness of our sensations. Still it requires an adjustment, and in the process we often encounter intense bouts of sleepiness.

In this state, known in the Buddha's teachings as "sloth and torpor," the mind becomes very heavy, dull, and unwieldy. There's often a feeling of boredom and disconnection from anything going on inside or outside of us. Feeling lulled to sleep while meditating, we get intensely drowsy and sluggish. At times there's a dreamy, drifting state of consciousness, but in this mental state there is not much awareness or energy. However, as soon as the promise of something exciting happens, such as the bell for lunch, all of our sleepiness disappears in an instant.

At one point in my early days of practice, when I was living in a monastery compound in India, I was given the instruction as part of my meditation practice to make a mental note of my predominant experience. Throughout the day, I was to note whether I was sitting, standing, walking, lying down, or whatever was happening most strongly. I began to notice that the single most common mental note I was making was "waiting." As I moved around the compound, I heard myself continually saying in my mind, "waiting . . . waiting . . . waiting . . . waiting. . . ." I finally said to myself, "What are you waiting for?" In that moment I realized I was waiting for something exciting enough or important enough or spiritual enough to happen so that I could make a mental note of it! I was living as though I were a tape recorder with the pause button on. I was waiting for life to happen—later.

Not being fully alive to what is happening right now is the ground of sloth and torpor. In meditation it manifests as sleepiness. In our daily lives, it can mean waiting for life to begin. We are capable of living much more fully than just waiting for something else to happen; life can be more than sleeping our way through to the next exciting event. In Burma, I finally found that the sitting and walking, sitting and walking, contained my most true and full experience. There was nothing more to wait for. In those "waiting" moments, my life had been actually flowering right in front of me. Until I stopped waiting for something else to happen, I just hadn't been able to see this. Learning to live our lives fully, awake to each moment, is the gift meditation practice can give us.

Restlessness

ON THE SURFACE, the meditation hall during a retreat looks like a haven of peace. But under the apparent calm, many storms and battles are proceeding as meditators unravel the workings of their own minds. One of the main hindrances in this process is restlessness, a powerful form of agitation in the mind. While each meditator sits in the present moment, the mind may be lost in anxiety about the past or the future.

I remember a retreat in my early meditation career. I was living in India and had decided with great certainty that I was going to live there for the rest of my life. I wanted this very much, but I was worried that the authorities might not allow it. And so I sat in meditation and planned exactly how I was going to accomplish staying in India forever. I thought, "Next year when I have to renew my visa, I'll go to that office, because I've heard that the visa officer there is very sympathetic to meditators, and I know that he will renew my visa. And then the year after that I'll go to this other place, because I've heard that the visa officer there is corrupt and will accept bribes. Then the year after that, I'll go to another place, because surely by that time, after having been in the country for two years, somebody will sympathize with my desire to stay. And then the year after that I'll go back to the first place. . . ." On and on it went. My mind was basically overtaken by anxiety. I would get up and do walking meditation, return to sit, and then review my plan all over again, convinced that it would not succeed unless I planned it out perfectly. This is restlessness.

Restlessness often comes from a desire to control that which is inherently uncontrollable. The inevitable agitation that arises when we do this causes us a great deal of suffering. From the Buddhist viewpoint, restlessness is a major hindrance because when our minds are filled with anxiety and obsessive thinking, it is impossible for us to see clearly.

Sometimes the mind may be overcome by anxiety about the past, rather than being lost in anxiety about the future. Very often in meditation practice, as we see more deeply into our psyches, memories begin to arise: things that we have done, or did not do, that caused pain to ourselves or others. Once when I was meditating in Burma with U Pandita, my interviews were scheduled immediately after Joseph Goldstein's. This meant that, as I waited in the back of the room, I ended up overhearing all of Joseph's interviews. One day, when he was speaking with U Pandita, he sounded dejected. He said to U Pandita, "I've been remembering something unskillful I did many years ago. It is terribly hurtful to recall it."

Joseph and I had been very close friends for about sixteen years at that point, and so I naturally became quite intrigued. Because we were on a silent retreat, however, it was months before I had the chance to ask him about this. Shortly after leaving Burma, I casually asked one day, "By the way, that day you were so unhappy, what was it you remembered that you had done in the past?" Joseph recounted an incident that had happened twenty-six years earlier.

A girl had invited Joseph to her Sweet Sixteen party, and he didn't feel like going, so he didn't. As it turned out, very few people went, and the girl was quite hurt. All of those years later her feelings of being rejected had begun to wash over Joseph as he was meditating. Even though it may seem like a little thing, sometimes just the memory of having created pain for another person, when it arises in the mind, can cause agitation and restlessness.

But we can no more control the events of the past than we can those of the future. Nor can we control memories from arising in our minds. But we can choose how to respond to the pain we feel over unwholesome actions that we might have committed. We may cling to them, caught in guilt and self-judgment, or we may forgive ourselves and move on.

An interesting distinction is made in Buddhist psychology between the state of remorse and the state of guilt. Remorse is considered a wholesome or skillful state of mind. We recognize that we have said something or done something that has created harm in some way, and we experience the pain of that. But because we essentially forgive ourselves, we can let go, and thus we have the energy, the inspiration, not to go on repeating the same mistakes. Guilt, on the other hand, is considered unwholesome or unskillful because of the component of self-hatred in it. We go over and over the harmful thing we have done, continually blaming ourselves, until we are drained. The result is that we are not left with the energy to transform our actions. Our minds then remain restless.

Whether restlessness is caused by anxiety about the future or about the past, the point of practice is liberation. In order to stop the cycle of pain, we can engage in skillful action. U Pandita's words to Joseph that day were: "The honest knowledge that you have done wrong is painful. You are your own best witness; you can't hide from yourself. Now it is time to move on; watch the painful feeling peacefully, without aversion, and your mind will find ease."

When I asked Joseph for permission to tell this story, he asked what point I hoped the story was going to illustrate. I answered, "How we can have strong remorse over just a little thing." He said, "It wasn't just a little thing. She was really hurt." No matter what the incident, creating pain for another hurts us, and it can result in restlessness of the mind.

It is important when we are encountering restlessness to expand our awareness to the unacknowledged feeling or emotion beneath the obsessive thoughts. The fact that we have not faced the anxiety or the guilt is what allows it to escalate into restlessness. Our task is to drop below the level of the repetitive thoughts and, mindfully and compassionately, experience what we are actually feeling.

This way we experience both relief and release, going beyond a habitual relationship to our pain. Ironically, we can even be filled with a great sense of comfort in the midst of pain. This is happiness that arises not from what is happening to us but from how we are relating to what is happening to us. We are relating to our feelings with the inner knowl-

edge, "It is okay. I do not have to run; I do not have to push
the pain away. I do not have to get lost in it. It is okay to
simply be aware of it."

This quality of relating openly to our feelings is the anti-
dote for restlessness, guilt, and anxiety. When we develop
the ability to open to our underlying feelings, we can transform guilt into wise remorse. Being aware of whatever we
are experiencing with a peaceful attitude allows us not to be
driven into restlessness.

Self-Forgiveness

THE POET RUMI SAID, "Pain will be born from that
look cast inside yourself, and this pain will make you go
behind the veil." When we clearly see the ways in which
we have hurt others, in that moment of recollection, we
experience pain. And this pain can become a tool for our
transformation. Going "behind the veil" of illusion, we stop
viewing ourselves as "bad" and open to the suffering nature
of the experience.

We know it can be terribly painful to recall the harm we
have caused others. I have sat in meditation with a woman
whose husband sexually abused their child for years while
she ignored her intuition with the thought, "It couldn't be
true." I have sat with a man who has beaten up women
when lost in rage, and with a man on death row who killed
someone twenty years before in the course of a robbery.
And I have sat with my own painful recollections of the
harm that I have caused others. No matter what the degree,
inflicting pain on another being inevitably results in experiencing pain ourselves.

We might think that reviewing a harmful action over and over in our mind with lacerating self-hatred counts as some sort of atonement, but actually compassion is atonement. When we are filled with guilt, our identity collapses, and we think, "This is who I really am, the one who . . ." As our sense of ourselves narrows in this way, we punish ourselves repeatedly through unhappiness, disconnection, loneliness, hopelessness. This is what we feel we deserve. We may even hear something like the Buddha's teaching that all living beings want to be happy and have the full potential to be happy, but it only makes us feel more isolated.

Many years ago, when I was sitting in meditation during a retreat, I found myself looking back at a difficult period of my life. I did not enjoy recalling some of my actions, but I found that as I began to see my behavior as part of an interconnecting flow of events, I could more easily view myself with understanding and forgiveness. I could see clearly how, as each event came into being, it created the ground for the next event to arise.

In the traditional teachings, an analogy is used to describe such an interconnected, causal sequence of events. When the great ocean swells with the tide, the rivers swell; when the rivers swell, the smaller rivers in the delta swell. When the ocean ebbs, the rivers ebb and the smaller rivers ebb. The moon's gravitational influence on earthly bodies of water is such that the waters, except in rare instances, act in concord with each other. With the arising of one thing, there is the arising of another that is linked to it. The existence of one event is conditioned by another. In the same way, all the elements of our existence—this mind and body, our internal and external worlds—are interdependent.

During the retreat, I saw that the events of my life, like the oceans and the rivers, had unfolded in a logical se-

quence. I saw that I had done the best I could in the circumstances as they were. Given the conditions leading up to
that time, there wasn't much likelihood that I would have
behaved in another way. Different behavior would have required a changed understanding that would have necessarily
been based on different information and experience.

We cannot undo what we have done, and we cannot escape the results of our actions. But rather than hate ourselves or dwell in helpless shame, we can dramatically
change the field in which our karmic seeds ripen by developing mindfulness and lovingkindness. This is the basis of
a spiritual life.

The law of karma, which is the moral and spiritual understanding of action, means that the intention or motivation
behind an action determines the kind of seed we plant in
each moment. This seed, given the right conditions, will
bear fruit sooner or later. But the law of karma does not
operate with mechanical rigidity. If the world were that
way, there would be nothing we could do to alter the course
of our lives. There would be no way to see the end of suffering and no point to spiritual life.

Just as nature allows for a multitude of variables in the
ripening of a seed, the seed of our intention does not exist
in isolation. The fruit resulting from an action depends not
only on the seed but also on all the characteristics of the
field in which the seed is ripening. Because we are continually re-creating the quality of influences in our lives, the
field in which our karmic seeds are taking root or ripening
is constantly changing. Thus, there exists the possibility of
a spiritual life and the opportunity to end suffering.

If we have done something inappropriate or unwholesome, and if our lives then become strongly influenced by
compassion, mindfulness, and lovingkindness, the field in

which our karmic seeds have been planted becomes radically altered, and this changes everything. This is a transformation that we can begin right now.

We start by using mindfulness and lovingkindness to look directly at the pain we have caused others and the pain we are experiencing ourselves. We look at our shame, our guilt, our fear, and our sadness with understanding and compassion. We see the difference between saying, "I am very wrong, and that is all that I am," and saying, "I did something very wrong, and I feel remorse about it." When we can experience the flow of our feelings with clarity, equanimity, and loving presence—not judgment and narrowness—our minds become like a mirror reflecting all that is arising. In the course of that process, the mirrorlike mind also reflects back its true nature: natural radiance, purity, and luminosity. As the Buddha said, "The mind is shining."

We can discover the capacity of the mind to be aware, to love, to begin again. Even though we might have acted unskillfully before, we discover the clarity and peace that are the essence of who we truly are, rather than the greed or anger or fear that motivated us to harm someone. It is not as if we have to do something to deserve this essence—it is simply natural to our being. We may have lived separate from it all our lives, but it has not gone away or dimmed. We may have dishonored it or violated its promise of wholeness, but it remains unchanged and is waiting for us to claim it.

When pain moves us to "go behind the veil" of apparent separation, we connect to the entirety of life and our place in it. Life accepts us; it is only awaiting our acceptance of ourselves. Forgiving ourselves does not mean condoning everything we have ever done, or imagining that the pain of recollection will simply go away. It means understanding the large web of conditions that helped create each action, and through that understanding, gaining compassion for ourselves and others.

Seeing Our Way through Doubt

FROM THE FIRST MOMENT I began to practice meditation, I felt as if I had come home. I never had any doubt about the benefits of the Buddha's teachings or the value of the practice of meditation. I did have doubts about other things: my own capacity to practice, whether my mind would ever quiet down, how much compassion I might ever experience. And for a while I had major doubts about which particular practice to do.

My first teacher was from a Burmese tradition, and so I practiced that method of meditation for some months. Then someone showed me a picture of a Tibetan lama. I was very intrigued and I decided to go meet him. He became my second teacher. It was a different tradition, a different lineage, and a different way of practice. Soon I found myself in a dilemma. I simply could not decide which practice to do. Whenever I sat down to meditate, I would obsessively think, "Should I do this one, or should I do that one? I bet that one is faster. Maybe this one is faster. Look at the people who do that practice. What do I think of them? What about the people who do this practice?" Whenever I was with my Burmese teachers, I asked them what they thought about Tibetan practice, and when I was with my Tibetan teachers, I asked them what they thought of Burmese practice. Dedicated to their own tradition, these teachers really knew very little about other practices, and the views they did offer were sometimes based on ancient, doctrinal disagreements.

In effect, I wasn't learning from either practice. Rather than meditating, I was sitting and ruminating about which practice would be best to do. Not knowing which was the "best" or the "right" practice, I couldn't even focus on an object of concentration. No sooner would I decide to follow my breath than I would begin to wonder if I shouldn't be saying a mantra or visualizing a deity instead. And rather than learning from my teachers what they knew very deeply, I insistently questioned them in areas they knew very little about.

The state of indecision I found myself in is one aspect of the hindrance of doubt. One of doubt's most significant and detrimental functions is that it prevents us from placing ourselves in an attitude of truly listening. It prevents us from allowing the truth to be revealed. Thus, when the mind is caught in doubt, when we believe our doubting thoughts and give them power, it is very difficult to progress in any practice.

Doubt makes it impossible to commit ourselves. We become unwilling to take the risk of giving a process some time, of allowing the truth to come forth. Instead of allowing answers to emerge intuitively, doubt demands that we know the answers immediately. Instead of drawing close to our experience, the doubting mind pulls us back from whatever the moment is offering so that we can scrutinize it—usually so that we can compare it to something else. And so we sit, thinking, "Am I doing it right? Am I doing it perfectly right? Is it worth doing? What am I doing here?" Continually comparing, judging, and assessing keeps us stuck and unable to see deeply for ourselves.

It is not that we should become gullible and simply be-

lieve everything we hear. It is both healthy and helpful to
have a certain level of skepticism about what we are told is
true. But when the Buddha urged his disciples not to simply
accept what he said without investigation, he meant that
doubt should impel us to discover the truth for ourselves.
If the truth is to become our own, we need to allow our
experiences to speak to us. And if we surrender to a process
long enough to experience it fully, then we are ready to
make a considered judgment: "What does it mean to me?
Is it worthwhile? Is it important? Is it useless? Should I forget it?"

Realizing that I had tied myself into a knot about which
practice I should do, I knew that I would have to unravel it.
I had to commit to one practice or the other. It hardly mattered which one I did, as long as I did it fully. I said to
myself, "Just do something. It doesn't have to be a lifetime
commitment. It doesn't have to be the absolutely right decision. Do it for six months, do it for a year, some period of
time in which to actually give it a try. Just do it and see what
happens." Immediately I was able to meditate again. I also
began once more to learn from my teachers by asking them
what they knew most about.

There are many ways to see through the hindrance of
doubt. One of the most effective is to actually use it as the
object of mindfulness—to recognize the confusion, the indecision, the questioning, not as authentic inquiry but simply for what they are: doubt. Seeing that, we can remember
again our real goal of insight. We can remember that our
chosen practice is a context in which we can allow the truth
to reveal itself. At times we may need to seek answers to our
questions from a teacher or through study, so that we can
come to understand what is healthy doubt and what is doubt
that just leaves us stuck. Sometimes, it's just a matter of

giving things time, as I had to do when trying to decide between forms of practice.

The most important tool in working with doubt is confidence in our own ability to see the truth. When I was no longer distracting myself with questions about which practice to do, I could face my deepest doubt, which lay below all of the superficial mental activity—whether I actually had the ability to fulfill the goals of the practice. In the hindrance of doubt, this kind of self-doubt is perhaps the most basic and most insidious.

"Self-efficacy," a contemporary psychological concept, is a quality that enables one to meet challenges as they arise. With self-efficacy we have faith in ourselves, in our ability to encounter difficulties. A person who has a strong degree of self-efficacy is willing to take risks, to face new challenges. This concept reveals that what we believe about our own abilities profoundly affects them. Our capacity to grow, understand, love, and connect is not a limited or defined quantity. But we limit it by what we believe about ourselves.

When self-doubt arises in the mind, we can transform it into a helping tool. We use it as a signal to cultivate confidence in our own ability to face obstacles that naturally arise on the path of discovery. This basic confidence enables us to face any level of doubt. Then we can experiment wholeheartedly, not holding parts of ourselves back from our practice and our lives.

The key to cultivating confidence in ourselves is understanding our right to make the truth our own. In a discourse in the early Buddhist canon, the Buddha addresses a group of villagers confused by the varied presentations of so many teachers, saying: "You should decide not by what you have heard, not by following convention, not by relying on the texts . . . and certainly not out of respect for a teacher.

When you know for *yourselves* that 'these things are unhealthy, these incline toward harm and suffering,' then you should abandon them. When you know for *yourselves* that 'these things are healthy, these incline toward welfare and happiness,' then having come upon them, you should stay with them."

When we realize that access to the truth is our natural birthright, we can overcome the doubt that seeks to separate us from our experience. Then we draw as close as possible to each moment, not with confusion but with wisdom.

Resting the Exhausted Mind

WHEN THE INSIGHT MEDITATION SOCIETY first opened, one of the teachers, Steve Armstrong, created a mock brochure that featured the brilliant motto: "It is better to do nothing than to waste your time." Although that motto never made it into our official presentation, it actually was an accurate description of insight meditation. Basically, we enter into mindfulness practice to learn how to do nothing so as not to waste our time or our lives. We learn how not to act out the habitual tendencies we generally live by, those actions that create distress for ourselves and others, and get us into so much trouble. Doing nothing (or what the Taoists call nondoing) does not mean shutting our minds off or going to sleep, but it does mean resting—resting the mind by being present to whatever is happening in the moment, without adding to it the effort of attempting to control it. Nondoing means being at peace.

In our usual mind-state, we are continually activating the process that, in Buddhist terminology, is known as *bhava,* which literally means "becoming." In this state of becoming, we are subtly leaning forward into the future, trying to have security, a feeling we can hold on to, trying to keep things from changing. We are continually out of balance in this state, as we even try to feel the next breath while the present one is still happening.

When Buddhist teachers talk about letting go, or abandoning, or renouncing, they are talking about dropping the burden of becoming and returning our awareness to the natural center of our being, returning to a state of natural peace. The movement that is uniquely helpful in meditation is to come back, to relax, to let go of leaning forward, to let go of grasping. We can relax even from the anticipation of our next breath. We settle back, return to the present, and return to ourselves. This is what is meant by nondoing.

Meditation is not the construction of something foreign; it is not an effort to attain and then hold on to a particular experience. We may have a secret desire that through meditation we will accumulate a stockpile of magical experiences, or at least a trophy or two, and then we will be able to display them for others to see. We may feel that we will increase our value as human beings by a process of spiritual acquisition, gaining more goodness and purity, acquiring enlightenment and understanding with a certain sense of ownership and possessiveness: "my enlightenment," "my clear understanding." Our typical consumer-culture mind wants to view enlightenment as performance art or as social cachet: "People will surely notice that I've been transformed."

Letting go of this burdensome desire for acquisition and performance, we can just let the mind rest in ease. As my teacher Nyoshul Khen Rinpoche puts it, "Rest in natural great peace, this exhausted mind." Then, rather than wast-

ing our time, our doing nothing can lead us into the insight-
ful and renewing rest of the timeless.

The Torment of Continuity

WHILE ON MY FIRST RETREAT with U Pandita, I
diligently wrote down brief notes after each period of sitting
and walking meditation. I did this so that I could describe
my meditation experiences clearly to him in our interviews.
I went in for one of my first interviews prepared to make a
presentation of my practice. As I began relating my meditation experiences, U Pandita said, "Never mind that. Tell me
everything you noticed when you put on your shoes." I said,
"Well, I didn't really pay tremendous attention to putting
on my shoes." He told me to try again, and that was the end
of the interview. I spent the rest of the day sitting, walking,
and paying especially careful attention when putting on
my shoes, noticing the intentions, the movements, and the
feelings.

The next day, I went into my interview ready to report
on my sitting, walking, and putting on of shoes, when U
Pandita said, "Tell me everything you noticed when you
washed your face." Sadly, I hadn't really paid any attention
to washing my face, and I had to say, "Well, I didn't notice
anything." My interview over, I went out to sit, walk, put
on my shoes, and wash my face, all very mindfully.

Every day U Pandita would ask me a different question.
Never knowing what he might come up with, soon I found
I was practicing mindfulness in everything I was doing—
putting on my shoes, brushing my hair, brushing my teeth,
washing my clothes, looking at my watch. At first it felt so

burdensome—every single moment, I had to pay attention. In my mind I began calling this retreat "the torment of continuity." However, soon I saw that the emphasis on continuity of awareness was a great gift. When I stopped resisting, it opened up a deep and clear understanding of what meditation actually is.

In traditional Buddhist teachings, there is a list called Nineteen Ways to Be Mindful, and it covers just about every action of the body you might perform in a day. Besides noting that you can be mindful while sitting, lying down, standing, and walking, the list includes details such as being mindful when you're moving forward or backward, seeing forward and seeing sideways; being mindful when you're intentionally stretching, and when you're bending your hands or legs or your body. It lists chewing food and drinking as times to be mindful. It includes putting on and taking off clothes, going to the bathroom, getting up from sleeping, opening your eyes. The list ends with being mindful when you have to talk and when you're keeping silent. The classical teachings indicate clearly that meditation isn't just about sitting and walking; meditation includes everything we do.

This practice that U Pandita had given me, the torment of continuity, actually became a great relief. Instead of feeling that I had to drop whatever I was doing and rush into the meditation hall to have a great experience, I realized that whatever I was doing was exactly what I needed to be mindful of. Whether drinking a cup of tea or formally sitting in the meditation hall, the practice was to be as present and aware as I possibly could. Stretching, bending, getting up, getting down, seeing, hearing, tasting. Every step I took toward the meditation hall was as important as anything I experienced once I was sitting on my cushion. I didn't have to look for a wonderful experience or an unusual feeling. Meditation became a way of life. By the end of that retreat, any concepts I'd had about true meditation happening only in formal practice had been completely overturned.

Something else of significance was laid to rest for me in this torment of continuity. Being mindful all the time meant there was no time to judge. I could no longer look back on a sitting, for example, and try to decide if it had been a good sitting or a bad sitting, because in the very act of getting up, I had to pay attention to what I was experiencing right then. If my attention wandered, as it tended to do, there was always something that was happening right in that moment to refocus on—a taste, a sound, a moment of bending, or the sensation of touch. There was no time to despair, thinking, "Where have I been? Why did I let that happen? What kind of a meditator am I?" Once the burden of judgment and evaluation dropped away, each moment became equally precious and important.

In the torment of continuity, I realized to the deepest level of my being that there is nothing needed outside of what is happening right now . . . and right now . . . and right now for the realization of mindfulness. Our goal is not in the distant future, it is right now, in whatever activity is happening.

Daily Liberation

MY COLLEAGUE Kamala Masters began her meditation practice with Munindra as her first teacher. When he went to Hawaii to teach, Kamala opened her house to him as a place to stay. At the time, she was a single mother, raising three small children alone and working two jobs to make ends meet. When he first arrived, Munindra strongly encouraged Kamala to set aside a portion of each day for formal sitting meditation. This is, after all, the traditional incantation of meditation teachers: "Sit every day, sit every day." Kamala kept pointing out to Munindra that there was no way in the world that she was going to have time to sit every day. Finally, perhaps seeing that her protest had reason, he asked her what she did more than anything else each day. She thought for a moment, then responded: "Wash dishes." Munindra went over to the sink with her, and together they practiced mindful dishwashing. Thus began Kamala's daily meditation practice.

Then Munindra noticed that in the short, dark hallway between Kamala's bedroom and the rest of the house, the children tended to leave her alone. He suggested that she consider the hallway her temple for walking meditation. Whenever Kamala was in that part of the house, she practiced mindfully walking those few steps. She says now that, because she was so aware there, she came to regard that hallway as a sacred site.

One of the most wondrous aspects of the Buddha's teachings is that they are never removed from a sense of humanity. Being a human being himself, the Buddha talked about what it ultimately means to be human and to be happy. The depth of the Buddha's compassion is reflected in the tremendous pragmatism of his teachings. He offers a path that is direct, present, and available throughout every aspect of a human life, not abstract or removed from normal people.

The basic principle of the Buddha's teachings is not to emphasize tradition but to point out our own capacity for insight and realization. They embody a completely living spirituality, which can be supported by tradition but never replaced by it. Rooted in simplicity and in connection, the path is about going beyond one's sense of limitation, joining into the vastness of life, and knowing liberation. The Buddha said that all of his teachings had one taste: the taste of liberation.

Our path, our sense of spirituality, demands great earnestness, dedication, sincerity, and continuity, but it is not intended to be a strained, hectic, or tortured pursuit. Above all, it is meant to be our own. It is a practice based in feeling at home in our own process, in ourselves, and in our unique situations, so that while we practice with effort and earnestness, we also practice with gratitude and ease. We can be natural even as we are wholehearted in applying the practice. We can put forth our complete effort while also being at peace. This ease comes from being uncontrived in our efforts and using every moment we can to see more clearly. Like Kamala mindfully washing dishes or walking down the hallway, our dedication to awakening can be expressed throughout the moments of our daily lives.

Part Two

The Practice of Transformation

THROUGH MEDITATION PRACTICE we learn to enter into silence, and there the fruits of the practice reveal themselves: wisdom, which is seeing deeply into the true nature of life, and compassion, the trembling of the heart in response to suffering. Wisdom reveals that we are all part of a whole, and compassion tells us that we can never really stand apart. Through this prism we see life with openness, knowing our oneness. We find wisdom and compassion coming to life, transforming how we understand ourselves and how we understand our world.

Like the Presence of the Sky

ONE DAY I ASKED an acquaintance of mine, "How
has your life changed since you started meditation practice?" Without a moment's hesitation, he said that before
starting to practice, whatever happened in his mind felt as
if it were taking place in a small, dark, enclosed theater and
that everything taking place on the stage seemed to be overwhelming and solid. He went on to say that now, since
he started meditation practice, his awareness of what happened in his mind was like watching an opera in an open-
air theater.

It was funny that he would use this metaphor of an out-
door theater. Not long before that conversation, some
friends had taken me to my first opera—in an open-air theater in Santa Fe, New Mexico. Our seats were situated so
that I could see both the stage and the sky all around it. In
New Mexico the sky is so vast. Watching the characters
struggling with the immense complexity of their lives
against the backdrop of that open and spacious sky was a
fantastic juxtaposition: however histrionic the event, however dramatic, however much despair or ecstasy was happening onstage, it was all in the context of that hugely
spacious sky.

Through meditation practice we begin to enlarge our
own perspective. We discover a quality of space that knows
no bounds, a quality of mind that can accept anything. The
practice is about nurturing this immensity of vision. Sometimes we think that what is in front of us is so solid and so
real, and yet it is actually just an operatic interpretation. If
we step back and see things in a greater perspective, our

experience changes completely. But when we aren't able to see this larger perspective, our energy and awareness tend to collapse around certain events. We habitually create, as William Blake put it, "mind-forged manacles," binding ourselves to limited perceptions.

However, we can retrain the mind to be aware, to be mindful, to take rest in what is actually happening, to relinquish grasping, aversion, and delusion, and to be filled with love. The mind has already been trained: to grasp, push away, separate, collapse, to be confused, to not see options. We have been trained to be jealous, anxious, doubtful, afraid, and to judge ourselves. Our minds have basically been conditioned to be stuck in the opera and to miss the sky above and around.

Training our mind through meditation does not mean forcibly subjugating it or beating it into shape; it means very patiently inclining the mind toward awareness, lovingkindness, compassion, letting go, and toward a generosity of spirit. Again and again, no matter what is happening, we incline the mind through meditation practice to relax and experience the spaciousness that is inherent to awareness and to lovingkindness. Ten thousand joys and ten thousand sorrows may arise—but that spaciousness, like the presence of the sky, is able to transform our lives.

Never Alone

LOVINGKINDNESS, or metta, is one of the main meditation practices of the Buddhist tradition. It's a practice that involves offering a sense of lovingkindness to oneself and then extending this offering to loved ones, friends, acquaintances, difficult people, and ultimately to all beings everywhere.

Once, when I was teaching a lovingkindness retreat, one of the students told me about the impact this practice had on her life. She said that the entire past year of her life had been filled with a great deal of loss and disappointment. It would have been easy for her to become disconsolate— except for one thing: her recognition that somewhere in the world somebody was offering lovingkindness to *all* sentient beings everywhere. By definition, that included her. Somebody somewhere, never having met her, not knowing her situation, not having any personal connection to her, was actually sending her thoughts of lovingkindness. Someone was opening his or her heart and wishing for her happiness, peace, safety, and freedom. This was happening simply by virtue of the fact that she existed; she was a sentient being, and that was enough for her to be a deserving recipient of the force of love. This recognition, she said, was the singular force that had given her the strength to go on, to keep her heart from breaking during difficult times.

How wonderful to know that there is always someone who is dedicating this very moment to generating love and compassion for you and for all beings. Without knowing anything about you, without knowing who you are, not because you are especially nice, not in exchange for any favor or out of obligation, but simply because you exist— someone right now is deeply wishing you well, wishing for your happiness. If, like the woman on the retreat, we can recognize this, then we realize that we are not isolated in our suffering. No matter what our particular circumstances, we are never completely alone—we are each receiving this force of beneficence. We can also recognize that when we practice metta, when we offer love and compassion, we are giving a true and powerful gift. Somebody somewhere is very gratefully receiving it.

Seeing Pain

MY PREDOMINANT EXPERIENCE when I first started practicing meditation was physical pain. Not only had I never meditated before, but I had never been able to sit cross-legged. Suddenly, there I was in India, expected to sit on the floor in the classical meditation posture. No chairs were provided, and this was before the advent of the meditation bench that supports a kneeling position. We did not even have specialized meditation cushions, such as *zafus*. I just sat on my rolled-up sleeping bag or on a pile of extra clothing.

I habitually carried a lot of tension in my body anyway, and when I first sat down, in only a semblance of the cross-legged posture, my knees were closer to my shoulders than to the ground. I experienced many levels of pain, not only from the unfamiliar posture, but from deeply embedded physical and emotional tension. It was a powerful revelation to see the thoughts and judgments that arose in my mind in response to the pain I encountered. They were a perfect reflection of my conditioned tendency to avoid looking at pain or any unpleasant experience.

Whenever pain arose while sitting in meditation—which was almost constantly—I immediately shifted my posture. Over time I began to observe that I didn't move because the pain was so intense or severe. I moved with the first mildly uncomfortable twinge, in response to certain thoughts that came up in my mind: "Oh, no, the pain is going to be like this the rest of the day." Or, "I'm going to be in pain like this every time I sit down to meditate for the rest of my life." Or, "I'm never going to make it to the end of the sitting period." I was making the assumption that what I was experiencing in the moment was only going to get worse. By letting that thought rule me, I was essentially adding minutes or days or a lifetime of anticipated pain to the present moment's pain. Trying to face it all at once, I felt helpless and overwhelmed. In fact, I could have borne quite well what was happening in any given moment, but my fears about the future made the suffering unbearable.

On top of this, I added comparisons between my experience and what I imagined that everyone else in the room was experiencing: "No one is suffering the way I am." I believed everyone else was having a pleasant, positive time meditating. These thoughts soon melded themselves into quite a negative self-image: "If you were a spiritually advanced person, there would be a free flow of energy throughout your body, with nothing cramped or twisted, and you wouldn't feel any pain. It is because you are so obstructed that you have pain." To what was actually a moderate degree of physical discomfort, I was adding a large degree of mental torment.

I finally came to realize that I had the same kind of conditioned reaction to any unpleasant experience, physical or mental—I wanted to move away from it, and I judged myself negatively for having it in the first place. These dynamics were occurring in my mind, unobserved, at other times, not just when I was sitting. Even the word *pain* was like a neon light glaring in my mind as something fearful, abhorrent, terrible—definitely to be avoided at all costs.

All of our lives we are taught to run from physical or psychological pain, or to disguise it, as if it were disgraceful.

We often believe that we should be able to make pain go away. Rarely do we sit down and, in an open, relaxed, non-judgmental way, genuinely explore the pain in our lives.

Meditation practice is a powerful tool for revealing our conditioned reactions to unpleasant experiences, allowing us to penetrate to their very depth. Opening to painful experiences does not mean a passive acceptance of pain. Rather, we learn to go to the heart of each moment's experience, even if it is painful, because there—unclouded by conditioning—we discover our lives. The effort to push away what is unpleasant, the tendency to project pain into the future and then feel overcome by it, the interpretations we add to it—all keep us from having a personal, direct, and intimate acquaintance with what we're actually experiencing. So, when we observe something like pain directly, we come to see its actual nature: like everything else, pain is a changing phenomenon with no inherent substance.

Eventually I found that my legs relaxed, my knees reached the floor, and I could sit for long periods of time with no pain. Yet I was, in fact, released from my terrible fear of the pain long before then, when I saw through the seeming solidity of the pain. Rather than viewing it as a monolithic entity taking over "my" body, I saw the pain as a kaleidoscopic world of ever-shifting sensations: tingling, tightness, heat, throbbing, and a thousand other qualities of sensation. These were what I had been lumping together and calling "pain." By seeing these component parts—all in essence coreless and ephemeral—I finally learned to explore the texture of pain rather than feeling crushed by it.

Just as important, I could take this lesson into an exploration of emotional pain as well, such as dejection. Like pain, we think of dejection as one "thing" that is solid and overtakes the mind. But when we can see it as it truly is—some moments of anger, some of mourning, some of sadness, and some of hopelessness; a composite of contingent reality, not solid and unchanging but fluid and dynamic within it-self—we do not need to feel so afraid of it. This is the essence of facing pain: by seeing it clearly, rather than running from it or judging ourselves for it, we become able to develop a radical new relationship to it. Then we can let go of our fear of pain and find ourselves.

Judging

EARLY IN MY PRACTICE I got the idea that really good meditators were continuously being bathed in a flood of white light. No one ever told me I had to experience this white light; somehow I just imagined that it was a sign of good practice. And I had a sneaking suspicion that as soon as I finally experienced white light, my teachers would bestow the truth upon me: "Finally," they would say, "we had almost given up hope that you would ever get here."

But I didn't experience any white light. I mostly had knee pain. As time went on and my practice deepened, I had many different experiences, but none of them were white light, and I really wanted that white light. No matter what I experienced, it wasn't good enough for me. "Where is the light? Why isn't it here?" This was my inner incantation. I felt contemptuous of my practice and judged it constantly, comparing it with what I thought should be happening. The heartache was tremendous.

In meditation practice, as in life, we might judge our difficult experiences—such as restlessness, negative mind-states, physical pain, and so on—as not being right, as being somehow out of place or worthless. We often try to prolong pleasant experiences, as though they are the only ones worth having. But with increased patience and insight, meditation practice can take us beyond these conditioned reactions.

When we meditate, we view whatever arises with acceptance and a spirit of generosity, with a mind that is open and spacious. The purpose of this acceptance is not to develop passivity but to get as close to our experience as we can. When we are free of our conditioned reactions, we are able to have an intimate, personal vision of what is true. The full range of what a human being can know and feel and want and fear is within each of us: the entire display of a human life. No matter what we are experiencing, being aware of it is the path to wisdom.

Once when I was sitting with U Pandita, I began to notice a recurring pattern in our interviews. Whenever I told him about a meditation experience that I thought was wonderful and impressive, his response was: "Did you note it?" In his tradition of practice, "noting" refers to placing a mental label on each experience, so as to know it more directly. But I would sit there and think, "What does he mean, 'Did you note it?' It was glorious; how could I have just noted it like everything else?" Other times I went to see him with doleful accounts of painful meditation experiences. He looked at me and said each time, "Did you note it?" I would think, "What does he mean, 'Did you note it?' It was awful; can't he understand that?" It took a while for me to appreciate the simplicity, and importance, of U Pandita's approach: he was asking me if I had been aware of each experience with spaciousness and clarity of mind. He was far less concerned with what was happening than with the quality of awareness I was bringing to it. What we want in practice is to understand the nature of our lives, and this does not demand a particular experience but a quality of awareness that excludes nothing.

Meditation is like going into an old attic room and turning on the light. It is not the fantastic white light that I had so much desired but the common, average, liberating light of awareness. In that light we see everything. We see all of the beautiful treasures that engender awe and gratitude for our ability to discover them. We see all of the dusty, neglected corners that inspire us to say, "I'd better clean that up." We see all of the unfortunate relics of the past that we thought we had rid ourselves of long ago. We see it all with an open and loving awareness.

The inclusiveness and intimate nature of mindfulness mirrors the nature of love. We discover the fact that awareness can go anywhere, and that we are capable of having a loving heart in any circumstance. This discovery is the wellspring of joy that meditation can bring into our lives. Loving awareness contains a strength that the judging mind can never give us.

The truth is everywhere, in all of our experiences. We do not have to fitfully try to have a sublime, magical experience and, in this effort, disdain what is actually happening. We do not have to struggle to find the truth. Every single moment is expressive of the truth of our lives, when we know how to look. As Saint Augustine said, "If you are looking for something that is everywhere, you don't need travel to get there; you need love."

Personality Types

I HAD a funny experience early one morning walking from my house to the Insight Meditation Society. As I walked by the place where I usually park my car, I noticed that the car was gone.

I thought, "That's strange, my car's gone. Why is that?" The night before I had gone to Cambridge to give a talk, and when I came back there was almost no gas in the car, so, not yet quite awake, I confusedly thought, "Maybe somebody took it to put gas in it." I went into the staff dining room, and the first person I saw was a staff person who, of anyone, was the most likely person to have taken the car. So I asked him, "Did you take my car?" And he said, "No, I didn't take your car." I said, "You didn't take my car?" "No," he replied, and I said, "Well, it's gone." And then he said, "Are you sure?"

Well, a car is quite a large object, so I said, "It really seemed to be gone. It looked altogether gone." But right away I started to doubt myself. I thought maybe it was there and I had just walked by it and didn't notice it. Then a friend who had overheard this exchange said, "You know, you probably lent it to somebody and you forgot." And I said, "Of course, I probably forgot." Then I thought, "Who could I have lent it to?" I couldn't think of anybody. So I spent much of the morning wondering what had happened to my car. When I went to lunch, another friend walked in and I asked her, "Did you take my car?" And she said, "No, I didn't take your car." Just then Joseph walked by and said, "Oh, I know what happened to your car." I asked, "What happened to my car?" He explained that *he* had lent the car to someone who needed it urgently, no other car was available, and there hadn't been an opportunity during the morning to tell me about it.

This whole exchange reminded me so much of the classical Buddhist system of personality types. In this system, I'm what's referred to as a deluded type, and I realized that my reaction to what had transpired with my car was a quintessential manifestation of that sort of personality.

For one thing, deluded types don't do well very early in the morning. So, I got very perplexed. Deluded types tend to lose confidence in their own perception and thus go spiraling in confusion with feelings of bewilderment and uncertainty. This is just what I had done with the missing car.

In response to any particular situation, some people tend to look on the bright side, some will naturally focus on what is wrong, and some will feel quite confused. These three responses conform to the three main character types defined in Buddhist psychology: the desirous or greedy type, the angry type, and the deluded type. While all of us are to some degree a mixture of all three types, many people do exhibit a strong predominance of one or another of these main characteristics.

For example, if you are a greedy type and someone tells you about the Buddhist system of personality types, you may carefully take in this information, thinking to yourself that this is a startlingly wonderful character typology, and that you are going to learn all you can about it. If you are an angry type, you might say to yourself, "How can everybody fit into three simple little categories. I hate this kind of thing. It makes me feel reduced to somebody else's idea of who I am." If you are a deluded type, you might feel a bit dazed by all this, wondering, "Which one am I?" Or, if you're a mixture of these types, your response may include an aspect of all of the above.

We can learn a great deal about ourselves as we explore this part of Buddhist psychology. Most important, we can learn that these are impersonal tendencies, which were identified thousands of years ago, and we don't have to identify with them or take them as an affront to our ego. They are simply conditioned tendencies of human character.

The *Visuddhi-magga*, "The Path of Purification," a commentarial work in the Theravadin tradition, describes each type in detail. Notice if anything in the following passage from that text seems familiar:

> When one of greedy temperament sees even a slightly pleasing visible object, they look long as if surprised. They seize on trivial virtues, discount genuine faults, and when departing, they do so with regret as if unwilling to leave.
>
> When one of angry temperament sees even a slightly displeasing visible object, they avoid looking long as if they were tired. They pick out trivial faults, discount genuine virtues, and when departing, they do so without regret as if anxious to leave.
>
> When one of deluded temperament sees any sort of visible object, they copy what others do. If they hear others criticizing, they criticize; if they hear others praising, they praise, but actually they feel equanimity in themselves, the equanimity of unknowing!

We probably all know that first type of person—one who has a hard time facing difficulties in any given situation and might almost insist on ignoring them; they just want things to be nice all of the time. We probably all know that second type of person, whose mind seems to seize on what is wrong in any situation, sometimes pointing out problems everyone else has missed (but not necessarily thinking they will be resolved!). And we probably all know that third type of person, who easily gets confused; uncertain about what they actually feel or perceive, they are somewhat dependent on the views of others. Again, all of us have aspects of all three tendencies, but sometimes one is more marked in our personality structure than the others.

Some people, as they read this, may smile with recognition as they immediately see themselves and others in the description of these three types. If not the *Visuddhi-magga*'s description of how each type tends to move and to sleep may ring a bell:

> You can discern the type of person by the posture. When one of greedy temperament is walking in their usual manner, they walk carefully, put their foot down slowly, put it down evenly, lift it up evenly, and their step is springy. One of angry temperament walks as though they were digging with the points of their feet, puts their foot down quickly, lifts it up quickly, and their step is dragged along. One of deluded temperament walks with a perplexed gait, puts their foot down hesitantly, lifts it up hesitantly, and their step is pressed down suddenly.
>
> When they sit or they lie down to go to sleep, one of greedy temperament spreads their bed unhurriedly, lies down slowly, composing their limbs and, they sleep in a confident manner. When woken, instead of getting up quickly, they give their answers slowly as though doubtful.
>
> One of angry temperament spreads their bed hastily anyhow. With their body flung down, they sleep with a scowl. When woken, they get up quickly and answer as though annoyed.
>
> One of deluded temperament spreads their bed all awry and sleeps mostly face downward with their bodies sprawling. When woken, they get up slowly, saying, "Huh?"

The commentary on the text contains many more such examples. Traditionally, this classification according to types was used for determining which kind of meditation practice might be most helpful for someone, and to aid people in taking their conditioned tendencies less personally. This information can lead to finding more balance in our lives. So, for example, to remedy a tendency toward anger, we practice lovingkindness. To ease grasping, we practice generosity or renunciation. To counteract delusion, we practice focused attention.

One type is not considered better than another; all are equally conditioned and impersonal. With mindfulness as the alchemical agent, each of these factors can be transmuted. It is possible to experience the positive aspect of each mental tendency, without compulsiveness or a sense of limitation. In the teachings, this is considered their purified form.

The tendency toward greed, for instance, also indicates a willingness to draw near to things, to experience life fully, to surrender to experience. So the purified manifestation of greedy types is faith. Faith too allows us to draw near to experience, to face life more fully, to surrender, and it does so without the stickiness and obscuring intoxication of greed.

Angry types may fixate on what is wrong in a situation, but this also contains an aspect of being ready to look more deeply than others might be inclined to, being willing to honestly recognize what may be unpleasant or unwelcome. Because of these factors, anger transmutes to wisdom. Wisdom also demands that we go beneath a superficial level of perception, that we be able to incorporate the unpleasantness that is normally hidden from view, and thus more fully understand all elements of life. Wisdom can function in these ways without the painful and isolating effects of anger.

The deluded type feels disconnected from whatever is

happening in a situation and doesn't quite know how to respond, but with increasing mindfulness, this type of person can transform that same tendency into one of spacious equanimity. Rather than being insensitive to what is happening, the person responds with serenity, which comes from being fully connected at all times because of the clarity of mindfulness.

Whichever type we may think we are, it is important to recognize that we are all entrapped in some way or another by our conditioned minds. Mindfulness is the agent of our freedom. Through mindfulness we arrive at faith, we grow in wisdom, and we attain equanimity. No matter which avenue we come by, our liberation is achieved through being mindful of every moment.

Tidal Wave

JOSEPH GOLDSTEIN and I were once teaching a retreat on the Big Island of Hawaii. One day, when I was leading the first meditation period after lunch, I kept hearing the phone ring in the office beneath the meditation hall. I knew that Joseph was out of earshot on the other side of the building, but I kept expecting a staff member to answer the phone. No one did, however, and as it kept ringing I began to think, "Something is going on; there must be something wrong." I ended the sitting period, went down to the office, and waited only a few moments before the phone rang again. It was someone from the Civil Defense Department of Hawaii saying that the largest tidal wave in history was expected that day! Because we were in a facility very near the ocean, we had about forty-five minutes to evacuate. They told me that we were about an hour away from the nearest safe location.

I said to the person on the phone, "You know, we have seventy people here, and we have only two vehicles. Any road out goes right along the coast. I don't think we're going to be able to get out of here in time." She said, "I'll get back to you."

A few minutes later she called to say that they were sending a bus, only to then call back again to say that there was no longer time enough to do so. She directed us to find shelter in the highest point possible. Since the land above the center was inaccessible, the safest place we could get to was only as high as the second story of our building. The largest tidal wave in Hawaii's history was about to hit us, and we couldn't get away or get much above sea level!

Stunned, I hung up the phone and went into Joseph's room to seek counsel. He was doing a group interview with some course participants. As I stood quietly in the back of the room for a moment, I heard one of them speaking with a lot of unhappiness about the knee pain he was experiencing in the sitting posture during meditation. I thought to myself, "Boy, if you think you've got a big problem with your knee pain, you just wait!" It is not that I haven't had knee pain in my own practice, because I have, and I complained about it too. Before taking that phone call I might have had a very different response to this person's experience. But at the moment I was bearing news of unseen danger, and I had a radically different sense of proportion because of it.

We ended up moving all of the belongings up to the highest point we could find in the facility, with no idea of how high the waters might reach. Then we meditated as we waited for the tidal wave. While we sat, time became elastic, with some minutes seeming like hours, and hours going by like minutes. It was a tremendously profound sitting, as everyone faced the possibility of dying, engulfed in ferocious water. Some people prayed, others cried, some were silent.

For me, every moment of letting go in that meditation period was like a mirror of my own death, with its imperative to let go of absolutely everything known. Every moment of grasping and leaning forward to capture the next moment was excruciating. Every moment of settling back and being only with the present moment was peaceful. I often thought of the man with the knee pain, wondering how he was doing.

In the end, nothing at all happened. The tidal wave had missed the island altogether. We quietly gathered our things and went back downstairs. For a while, everyone functioned with the perspective born of unseen danger. And we all had a radically different feeling about our knee pain and about the ordinary difficulties of our lives. For a while, everybody woke up to the things that mattered most to them; and everyone felt grateful for what had sustained them when they were afraid and uncertain.

We practice meditation to support that radical perspective, for it is the truth. Our lives are fleeting and uncertain; most of us do not know how or when we will die. We practice meditation because, rather than grasping for what we do not have, or trying futilely to hold on to what is changing, we can instead settle into the moment and know the refuge of letting go. We practice meditation so as not to waste our precious lives.

The Greatest of Powers

I REALIZE it may be hard for some people to believe, but it is said that my teacher Dipa Ma could bake a potato in her hand and, even better, make it taste just like chocolate. She could walk through walls. She was known to duplicate her body and demonstrably be in two places at once. Sometimes, walking through the streets of Rangoon at night, she materialized a companion for herself. She also spontaneously appeared out of nowhere for appointments with her teacher.

Dipa Ma could read your mind and reveal what you kept hidden in your heart. One time she looked one month into the future and described the exact content of a speech that U Thant, the secretary-general of the United Nations, was going to deliver. She could send her mind to different realms of existence and back thousands of years to hear the Buddha give a talk. She could do many things we normally consider unbelievable.

Dipa Ma never used these powers for public display, but at times they became one of her teaching tools with people she trusted. She always used them without fanfare or egotism—rather, like a natural, almost casual offering of a very different perspective on things. Witnessing such phenomena certainly expanded our notions of the universe and the boundaries of life. They revealed a far bigger world than I had imagined.

Phenomena such as these psychic powers happen within the laws of nature. They are considered paranormal only because our definition of what is normal is very limited. Even with a slight expansion of our understanding, we push against usual definitions of the laws of nature. We have, for instance, learned to play at the edge of gravity, and thus we routinely fly from place to place and even explore outer space. The level of psychic powers that Dipa Ma demonstrated result from the mastery of concentration.

In Buddhism, concentration is considered to be the path of power, because as we concentrate, all of our usually scattered energy comes together into wholeness. The more we concentrate, the more energy returns to us, and this energy empowers us. With highly developed concentration, it is possible to experience that moment or pivotal point where conventions of time and space, matter and solidity first arise. At that point, the world is very malleable.

However, because psychic phenomena happen through power of mind rather than through wisdom, they are not considered ultimately freeing. This is why students are encouraged not to be seduced by them. Munindra taught these practices to Dipa Ma because she had a natural concentration, and because they are ancient practices he wished to revive. Most important, he taught them to Dipa Ma because he knew her purity of heart, and that she wouldn't misuse them. All the while he was guiding her in developing these powers, he held their attainment in clear perspective, saying, "These powers are not important. Enlightenment is important. These powers can bring one's downfall if used wrongly, if used with ego, thinking that 'you' are the one that is powerful. These powers are little things. It is fun, like magic. It is not important. Wisdom is important."

While these powers may seem remarkable and highly advanced, the path of concentration does not necessarily purify our view of the nature of life, our vision of the truth. Concentration may not clarify our sense of who we are and what our lives are about. It's through the development of wisdom that we discover the true nature of our minds, of our thoughts and feelings. Paying very careful attention, we see that the body and the mind, which have seemed solid and defined entities, are actually a bubbling, dancing, constantly changing flow of events. We see that this mind and body, while distinguishable, are also inseparable and interdependent. We see how the body affects the mind and the mind affects the body, in a great interplay of being. We see the laws of interdependence in the world around us and realize we are joined to all in this immeasurable flow we call life. Recognition of our interdependence brings forth unfabricated lovingkindness.

Through mastery of concentration, we might find the natural world more vast than we have supposed it to be; we might be able to play in the world in an extraordinary way, but that is not the freedom our practice intends. U Pandita's translator, struggling to express these concepts in English, once said, "One can have all these powers and do all these amazing things and still be a . . . um, um, . . . a loser." True freedom is the fulfillment of wisdom and boundless compassion. Our ability to see clearly and love fully are the greatest of powers. Dipa Ma was adept in both the path of power and the path of wisdom. And even though she had such extraordinary psychic powers, whenever I think about her, what I recall as most remarkable is that she was empty of self, and the most loving person I have ever met.

Your Last Apple

ONE OF THE FIRST MEDITATION instructions my teacher Munindra gave me was to be with each breath as though it were my very first breath and as though it were my last breath. I was to be with each step, each sound, each taste in just this way. Practicing in this spirit allowed me to bring a fullness and an immediacy of attention to each moment of my meditation. The fragmented aspects of my self came together. I was no longer so tempted to compare the present to what had happened in the past, because where was the past if this was my first breath? And if this were my last breath, I certainly could not postpone giving it my full attention, lost in the hope that something better might happen later on. I was not so inclined to experience the present with judgment, because how could I judge what I was going through without bringing in the past or the future? It is a beautiful and powerful way to practice—as well as a beautiful way to live and to die.

If we live without a sense of immediacy in our awareness, we seek fulfillment outside of ourselves, grasping at passing experiences. It becomes easy to fall into addiction to increasing levels of stimulating sensations. These supply us with a sense of wholeness, but it is a false wholeness held together with only passing phenomena of the external world.

Imagine doing something very simple, perhaps something that you have done many times before, so it does not arouse a compelling interest—something such as eating an apple. If you eat the apple while paying very little attention to the sight of it, the feel of it, the smells and tastes of it, then eating the apple is not likely to be a very fulfilling ex-

perience. Becoming aware of a mild discontent with the experience, you might start to think there is something wrong
with the apple, or perhaps that you didn't actually want an
apple after all. You may begin to think, "If only I could have
a banana, then I would be happy." But if you find a banana
and then eat it, again in a distracted or inattentive way, you
will again end up feeling unsatisfied. Instead of realizing
that you simply were not paying attention to the experience
of eating the banana, you might start to think, "My life is
just too prosaic; it is so ordinary. How could anybody be
happy with apples and bananas? What I need is something
exotic. I will be happy if I go out and get something unusual
like a mango." Then, perhaps with difficulty, you acquire a
mango. The first few bites may be a wonderful and fresh
sensation. Soon, however, you are finishing off the exotic
mango in just the same way you ate the prosaic apple and
banana, and once again you are left with a feeling of dissatisfaction.

It is rare for any of us to imagine that the quality of our
attention might play a role in our feeling unsatisfied, but it
is only when we are mindful that we find satisfaction in our
lives. Mindfulness is the key to life itself. When we relate
fully to our experience, we see that our perceptual world is
actually teeming with extraordinary sensations. It is as
though we are experiencing each thing for the very first
time.

Being mindful of sense pleasure is very different from
getting lost in attachment to it. Attachment does not make
a pleasant sensation more pleasant. Attachment actually di-
minishes our enjoyment, as we are inevitably anxious about
any potential change in the wonderful situation. On the
other hand, when we are mindful of the pleasure, we do not
need to grasp for the next great moment. Nor do we need

to postpone our feeling of happiness until a more exciting or more pleasing object comes along, thinking, "This isn't so nice because it would be better if . . ." Mindfulness allows for whatever is there.

Actually, we cannot know if the breath we are taking this very moment will be our last breath, or if we are eating our last apple, or hearing our last birdsong. By being aware—as though each experience were the last—we emerge from the half-dead world of disconnection and move into the profound and timeless satisfaction that is itself the fruit of mindfulness.

Moments of Liberation

My teacher U Pandita once said to me, "Do you believe what the Buddha taught, that every moment of mindfulness is a moment of freedom?" I said, "Oh, yes, I really believe it." And then he said, "Don't you think it might be better to actually realize it rather than just believe it?"

I said, "No doubt."

His comment in fact did reduce my doubt in the possibility that I could attain liberation, and it brought me face to face with this very potent teaching of the Buddha's: that being mindful, we can in any moment experience freedom. When we realize this in our own lives, we understand that whatever experience we are having, whether painful or pleasant, is worth our attention because it is an opportunity for freedom. What frees us in that moment is the power of awareness, regardless of the object of that awareness. Mindfulness itself loosens whatever bonds there might be.

In one of the great paradoxes of our lives, it can be said that suffering as well as freedom from suffering can arise right here and now, taking form in this body and in this mind. Two Pali phrases are used to express this paradox: *klesa bhumi* and *panna bhumi*. *Bhumi* means place of occurrence, place of arising. *Klesa* refers to those qualities that torment us and bring a strong degree of unhappiness. And *panna* means wisdom. The bhumi is always present in the form of our bodies and minds; what separates klesa from panna is mindfulness. With mindfulness, body and mind serve as the ground for liberation and freedom; without mindfulness, the very same body and mind become the foundation for torment. The Buddha's teachings point out to us that even the most ordinary person who walks on the path can succeed, because the basic material for liberation is already in all of us. We just have to choose whether we cultivate wisdom or suffering.

The traditional metaphor used to illustrate this is that of a garbage pail made of copper. Because it is a garbage pail, we tend to either overlook it or feel disdainful toward it. We then imagine the very same copper being fashioned into jewelry. Now we view the copper with appreciation, and even longing. Then, take that same copper and form it into statues of gods and goddesses that become objects of veneration. The material is identical, but when it is used differently, our reactions change accordingly. In the same way, rather than disregarding the experiences of our own bodymind, it is possible—in any moment—to regard them as the material for liberation.

All along the spiritual path we develop an ability to be calmer and to live more harmoniously. We lay bare our suffering and learn self-acceptance and compassion. We concentrate the mind and unveil our true nature. And all of this converges on perfect liberation, or nirvana. This is not a distant goal, as it may seem to be; every moment that we experience without grasping, aversion, or delusion is a moment of nirvana. It could be this moment.

The Web of Connection

A BRILLIANT and well-known image in the teachings of Buddhism is that of Indra's Net. The image depicts the universe as a net of infinite proportions. At each interlacing point, where the strings of the net meet, there is a multifaceted, highly reflective jewel, like a diamond or a piece of crystal. Each jewel reflects the others, including the reflected images held in the others. To look at one jewel, at one point, is to see the reflection of all jewels, at all points.

I was recently reminded of this image of Indra's Net when I visited the Holocaust Memorial Museum, Yad Vashem, outside of Jerusalem. One of the most moving and powerful places in the complex was the children's memorial, built by the contribution of an American couple whose son had died in a concentration camp in Germany. The memorial is a very dark chamber in the shape of a dome. As you enter, you are unable to see anything around you, so you grope your way through the darkness by holding on to a railing around the circumference. As you walk, you hear the names of children who died in the Holocaust slowly being read aloud.

In the center of the dome is a flickering candle. Lining the walls of the dome, hundreds of mirrors reflect this light from the candle in the center as well as its reflection in other mirrors. The impression is one of being surrounded by limitless points of light, each one representing a child killed in the Holocaust. As my mind became still, awed by this revelation, I began to feel that I too was among the reflections; I too was a part of this whole web of connection and relationship. Just as I could not separate myself from all the points of light, I could not separate myself from the lives and deaths of all those many children who had died. I had entered Indra's Net. Or perhaps more accurately, I had awakened to the reality of Indra's Net.

When we look at others, we see ourselves as well; when we look within ourselves, we discover all beings and all things in the universe. Every event, every entity, every mind-state, every experience we have is born out of a web of interconnectedness. We ourselves are born in every moment out of a web of interconnectedness. A vast multiplicity of causes come together, ceaselessly, to produce what we call ourselves, what we call life. In the children's memorial at Yad Vashem, I did not stand apart from what had happened in the Holocaust, nor from all of existence. In all of existence there is no one and no thing that stands apart.

Changing Seasons

ONE YEAR, one of my friends who lives in California planned a visit to New England in the autumn. Anticipating her arrival, I looked anxiously at the resplendent, colorful leaves on the trees, hoping they would stay the way they were. I so much wanted the trees to remain beautiful for her, I felt like I wanted to stick the leaves on them so that they would still be there when she came. I thought, "It has got to be this way when she comes, because if the leaves fall and they're all brown and shriveled, what kind of an inaugural autumn visit will that be for her?" As it turned out, she wasn't able to visit after all. When I heard that, I thought, "Well, I guess now I can just let nature take its course."

Of course, it's ludicrous to try to keep leaves from falling from the trees. But look at how much of our lives is spent trying to do the same thing in other ways, how often we try to keep things from changing. Yet, impermanence is the very fabric of our lives. It's not just that our lives are always changing; our lives are made up of change.

When we look at the natural world, we see so clearly that seasons come and go. Likewise, we can see that people come and go in our lives. We know that we have possessions and that they break or are given away, or we no longer care for them, or we might not notice and appreciate them anymore. We know that we might feel one way in the morning, another way in the afternoon, and perhaps yet another way at night. We know that at the end of our lives we die.

The practice of meditation makes us especially sensitive to how our perceptions themselves are constantly changing. There is a thought, and then it is gone. A sound arises and passes away. Smells and tastes and touch sensations come and go. Sights come into existence and vanish. Any moment of our lives can be seen, in Ralph Waldo Emerson's words, as "the volcanic present." Through meditation we come to know, not just poetically or lyrically, but actually, that we are dying and being reborn in every moment.

Sometimes in meditation practice the mind naturally alights on the aspect of being reborn in every moment. It is very beautiful. We notice the beginnings of things, the arising of objects. Whether a sound, or a feeling in the body, or an emotion, the most noteworthy aspect to us is its coming into being. We are experiencing the world and ourselves emerging, renewing, beginning again—and it is glorious. We are witnessing the magic that is life arising.

Sometimes it is quite different when we experience the truth of impermanence. The mind naturally alights on the endings of things, the moment-to-moment passing away that is the other face of change. We notice the dissolution of everything we experience. We become aware of the passing of everything that we hold dear, everything that we have tried to preserve and prolong. We turn to look at something, and it vanishes. We start responding to a feeling, then we notice it has already gone. Everything is so fragile, so evanescent, here and yet fleeting, revealing the seeds of its death right at the heart of its birth. Where is anything that we can hold on to? As Kalu Rinpoche said, "Life's breath is like a water bubble."

Even though seeing the arising nature of things is wondrous, and seeing the fleeting nature of things can be very disconcerting, both are essential. Opening to both aspects of change helps us to see the truth of how things are. Whether we like changing seasons or not, we learn to trust them, to sense the rightness of the cycles. Understanding the truth of change in our own lives, we can live with that same sense of trust and rightness.

One Thing Only

A FRIEND OF MINE once had to explain to her four-year-old son that the woman who had been providing child care for him since he was born was going to move away. Because her child was very attached to this person, my friend carefully told him about this step-by-step, making sure to say that the caregiver loved him, that they could write and talk on the phone and visit, but that she was going to move away and go live with her sister. The little boy listened carefully, then said to his mother, "Mommy, tell me that story again but with a different ending."

There are times in our lives when we too wish we could change the ending of the story. Sometimes we lose what we care about, we are separated from those we love, our bodies fail us as we get older, we feel helpless or hurt, or our lives just seem to be slipping away. These are all aspects of *dukkha*, one of the principle teachings of the Buddha. *Dukkha* means suffering, discontent, unsatisfactoriness, hollowness, change.

The Buddha said, "I teach one thing and one thing only: suffering and the end of suffering." Suffering, in his teaching, does not necessarily mean grave physical pain but, rather, the mental suffering we undergo when our tendency to hold on to pleasure encounters the fleeting nature of life, and our experiences become unsatisfying and ungovernable.

When I was first in India and heard the Buddha's teaching on suffering, I felt as though I were being handed a precious gift. Finally, someone was speaking openly about how things really are. Suffering does exist. While there is great pleasure in this world, there is also a great deal of pain. There are wonderful times of coming together, and there are also partings and losses. There is birth and also death. I felt as if I were hearing the truth for the first time—a truth that no one else had wanted to talk about.

When any of us tries to close the door on this truth, we create suffering. In our society the door is often shut because we are taught that suffering is shameful. We may close the door ourselves because we do not want to see our own suffering or reveal it to others.

This denial of suffering often occurs in family life. Sometimes there is great suffering in a family—discord, conflict, insecurity, violence—and in an effort to shield children from the truth, a great silence descends: the silence of denial, and of avoidance. If it is ever talked about, the suffering is repackaged and manipulated to look like something else. When talking about painful situations with children, skill and appropriate communication are called for, yet it is often the case that they are already well aware of what is actually going on. Without external affirmation of what a child feels to be true, a split arises within—a conflict between what the child is told and what the child knows intuitively. Children learn not to trust themselves, let alone trust their parents. Because of patterns like this, acknowledging the truth of suffering is an enormous liberation for all involved.

But the Buddha did not just teach suffering, he taught the end of suffering. A friend of mine, upon hearing the Buddha's famous statement about teaching one thing only, commented, "Suffering and the end of suffering are two things, not one thing." From one point of view they are clearly two—either we are suffering or we are free. We know the difference in our bodies, in our hearts, in the marrow of our bones. However, when we look deeper into this teaching, we begin to unfold its integrity. For in any experience, even a painful one, we can find the end of suffering right in the heart of the moment.

Yet when we are face to face with suffering and can't change "the end of the story," then how does suffering end? This is one of the most difficult situations we can encounter in our lives. We begin by not denying the pain, by acknowledging the truth of suffering. We do not become resigned to it or apathetic; we look at the suffering and discover the immense capacity of our hearts to include all aspects of life in our awareness. When we experience this immensity of heart, we recognize that it is not actually the pain itself that is unnatural and cruel, but the loneliness of feeling alone in the pain.

When we open ourselves to this fully, it becomes possible to touch an essential truth about life itself: suffering of one kind or another is a natural part of existence. Knowing this truth gives our lives wholeness and peace, as it frees us from the exhausting postures of pretense and denial. Sometimes when we open to suffering and see the roots of it, we also see the actions we might take to ease the suffering. For instance, my friend's young son suffered much less because of his mother's care and support. In this way, the path to the end of suffering includes clearly seeing the pain and replacing denial with awareness and compassion.

Countless times when I was with my teacher U Pandita, I said to him, "Things are really bad. My knees hurt, my back hurts, my mind is all over the place; I can't practice." So many times he listened and then simply responded, "This is dukkha, isn't it?" Over and over I sat before him, looking at him with enormous expectation, waiting for him to suggest the magic solution—anything that would make the difficulties all go away. As I waited, all my hope and fear evident, he just repeated, "This is dukkha, isn't it?"

While disappointing at first, U Pandita's response eventually became very liberating. Nothing I could do or change was going to compare to the power and freedom of first openheartedly recognizing, "This is dukkha." Essentially, U Pandita's words led me to the understanding that my difficulties weren't just a personal drama, but an opening into an aspect of life. Suffering must be seen and acknowledged, not for the sake of immersing in it, or getting lost in it, but in order to be more fully open to the truth, and to all beings.

There are times when we cannot change "the end of the story" and make all the suffering go away. But the end naturally changes as we relate to the truth before us with awareness and compassion. This is the one teaching of the Buddha: the truth of suffering is also the path to the end of suffering.

Facing Suffering

DURING MY FIRST VISIT to India in 1970, I saw many shocking things. The most shocking experience I had was when I found myself walking down a street in Bombay where young women were displayed in zoolike cages to be sold as prostitutes. Many of them were children who had been sold by their relatives to the criminal organizations who control the sex trade in India, so that the children's families would not starve.

The memory of that scene is still vivid in my mind—a horrible portent of things to come. Now, twenty-five years later, Bombay has an estimated 100,000 prostitutes, and the rate of HIV infection is over 52 percent. HIV is spreading so rapidly throughout the country that the United Nations estimates that India will soon lead the world with the largest population of people who are infected with the disease. The tide of suffering is already inconceivable, and it seems certain to get worse.

The rapidity of the spread of HIV in India is being brought about by many factors. Pervasive poverty means that even government hospitals frequently run short of supplies, so that needles and syringes are often reused at great risk of further infection. The powerlessness of women in

the culture means that prostitutes who ask men to use con-
doms might well starve, and wives who do so might be
beaten or simply put out on the street. So, the anguish only
grows.

One of the primary conditions for the growth of suffering, in India or anywhere else, is denial. Shutting our minds
to the experience of pain, whether in ourselves or others,
only ensures that it will continue. Yet when we witness immense suffering, and do not deny it or find some way to put
it out of our minds, it can seem overwhelming. I remember
walking down that street in Bombay, seeing those girls, feeling helpless, wanting to do something but not knowing
what.

In order to do anything about the world, we first must
have the strength to face it without turning away. By just
walking down that Bombay street, I faced a lot: the suffering
of women and children, the suffering of unimaginable poverty and disease, the suffering of ignorance, the suffering of
being able to help only a little bit when so very much needs
to be done, and the suffering of not knowing what to do.

In India there are not as many closed doors that hide
anguish, but the most crucial door, anywhere in the world,
is in the mind. By opening to the pain we see around us
with wisdom and compassion, we start to experience the
intimate connection of our relationship with all beings. The
Reverend Martin Luther King Jr. said,

> In a real sense, all of life is interrelated. All persons are
> caught in an inescapable network of mutuality, tied in a
> single garment of destiny. Whatever affects one directly
> affects all indirectly. I can never be what I ought to be
> until you are what you ought to be, and you can never be
> what you ought to be until I am what I ought to be. This
> is the interrelated structure of reality.

When we recognize the truth of interrelatedness, we are moved to act in ways that can make a difference. And whatever action we take, however insufficient it might seem, stands as testimony to our willingness to make someone else's yearning for release part of our own.

The truth of our interconnection—of how our suffering and our freedom from suffering are intimately interwoven with that of others—is present at all times for us to see, if we are open to it. It is present in the worldwide spread of AIDS, a disease that knows no boundaries. The first time I heard of AIDS, it was an exotic and rare disease and it was unimaginable that I would ever know anybody who would die from it. Now I have several friends who are suffering from AIDS, and several who have died because of it. There are few people anywhere on the planet whose lives have not been touched in some way by this disease.

So, in some subtle but very real way, I see that my own suffering and freedom from suffering are clearly interwoven with being willing to face the pain of those caged children in Bombay, as well as facing my own disquiet in becoming aware of their situation. The shift in my worldview to include them—rather than ignore them or reject them as not having anything to do with me—is the same shift in perspective that dispels our deeply held mirage of isolation.

In the delusion of separation, we may sense an oasis of connection to just a few people, maybe just our families and friends. We may create a fence around the oasis to protect and defend it, then a fort, and ultimately a whole way of life perpetuates the illusion. We get lost in feelings of disconnection and a sense of the futility of caring. It is only by not denying reality that we move into a knowledge of our interconnection with the whole of life. When we relate with wisdom and compassion, there we find true shelter in a community of all beings. Opening to the suffering of others may bring us uneasiness, but we, and potentially the world, are transformed by that opening. We become empowered to respond to the suffering with an unfathomable love, rather than with fear or aversion. Only love is big enough to hold all the pain of this world.

Faith—to Place the Heart Upon

THE WORD for faith in Pali is *saddha*. While sometimes translated as "confidence" or "trust," the literal meaning of *saddha* is "to place your heart upon." When we give our hearts over to a spiritual practice, it is a sign of confidence or trust in the path we have embarked upon. Faith opens us to what is beyond our usual, limited, self-centered concerns. In Buddhist psychology, faith is called the gateway to all good things, because it sparks our initial inspiration to practice meditation and also sustains our on-going efforts. Faith empowers us to move toward compassion, lovingkindness, and freedom.

Yet the concept of faith can be difficult for some people. Faith may be associated with mindless belief, or it may imply the need to proclaim allegiance to a creed or doctrine. Then we fear being judged, by ourselves or by others, for our degree of compliance. When we use the word *faith* in a Buddhist context, it is quite different from this. And this difference is crucial.

To "place the heart upon" does not at all mean to believe in something so rigidly that we become defensive about opening our minds to new ideas. Nor does it mean that we use what we have faith in as a way of feeling separate from and superior to others. We do not need to subjugate others because of our faith, or declare the vessel of our faith as the one true vessel. When we talk about saddha, we are talking about a heartfelt confidence in the possibility of our own awakening.

Faith does not need to be viewed as a fixed, solid thing that we either have or don't have. We experience faith on many levels. In a classical Buddhist text entitled *The Questions of King Milinda*, a monk named Nagasena uses an allegory to illustrate this. A group of people, gathered on the edge of a flooding stream, want to go to the far shore but are afraid. They do not know what to do, until one wise person comes along, assesses the situation, takes a running leap, and jumps to the other side. Seeing the example of that person, the others say, "Yes, it can be done." And then they also jump.

In this story, the near shore symbolizes our usual confused condition, and the far shore is the awakened mind. Inspired by witnessing another, we say "Yes, it can be done." This is one level of faith. But after we have jumped ourselves, when we say "Yes, it can be done" because we know it from our own experience, then we have entered into quite another level of faith.

The first instance is an example of what is called "bright faith." This is the kind of faith that happens when our hearts are opened by encountering somebody or something that moves us. Perhaps we are inspired by a person's qualities of wisdom or kindness. Whether it is someone we know or a historical figure, like the Buddha or another great being, we begin to sense the possibility of a different, happier way to live.

Bright faith is a wonderful feeling and an important beginning, but it is also unreliable. We might encounter one teacher one day and another teacher another day, and be moved powerfully by each of them, but in different directions. If we are looking for someone outside of ourselves to sustain our faith, we can easily become distracted by whatever influence comes into our lives next.

The deeper level of faith is called "verified faith," meaning that it is grounded in our own experience. This is a mature faith, anchored in our own sense of the truth, centered in an understanding of the nature of the mind and body that we come to through our own awareness. The inspiration and confidence we feel, rather than coming from something outside of ourselves, arises from within, and it fuels further inquiries into our own understanding.

It is a great turning point in our lives when we move from an intellectual appreciation of our spiritual path to the heartfelt confidence that says, "Yes, it is possible to awaken. I too can." A tremendous joy accompanies this confidence. When we place our hearts upon the practice, the teachings come alive. That turning point, which transforms an abstract concept of a spiritual path into our own personal path, is faith.

Selflessness

WHEN MY TEACHER Dipa Ma came to the United States for the first time, I took her with me to all of the places one would normally visit in a day: the supermarket, the gas station, the bank. She always expressed amazement at the abundance and the efficiency of the Western world. Dipa Ma was one of the most extraordinary teachers I have met; she exhibited a profound understanding of life. Yet, when it came to matters of the modern, technological world, she actually had little experience; still, her childlike insights taught me many wonderful lessons.

At one point, a friend needed to get some cash, so we walked to an ATM machine outside of a bank. He pushed in his card, punched in his code, and his money came out. We turned to Dipa Ma, expecting an awed reaction. Instead, she shook her head and said, "It's so sad, so sad." Confused, we asked, "What is so sad?" She said, "That poor person who has to sit behind the wall all day long, with no air, no sunlight, and has to pick up people's cards, count the money, and hand it out." Then we explained that there was no person behind the wall; it was just an interdependent process of component parts coming together. "Ah," she said, "It's like anatta."

In Buddhist teachings, the concept of anatta, or selflessness, means that there is no little being inside of us pulling the strings, no separate entity that receives sensory impressions, decides on a reaction, and then expresses it. In this world of incessant change, there is no enduring entity we can lay claim to and call "I" or "me" or "mine." Following the laws of nature, anything that arises in this mind and body does so as the result of various conditions coming together. Our lives are the continually changing process of our bodies and minds in interaction with the ever-changing elements around them. Yeats expressed this when he asked, "How can we know the dancer from the dance?" Our lives are the dance, and where is the dancer apart from that? This is the characteristic of anatta, which is variously translated from Pali as "insubstantiality," "essencelessness," or "transparency."

Some people ask: If there is no I, no me, no one behind the process, then who is reading? Who is meditating? Who gets angry? Who falls in love? If there is no self, who has memories? Who gets up and walks out of the room? Who dies? Who is reborn? In order to answer these questions, we have to see how we use the word *self* as a conceptual framework. Thinking of the self in this way is very useful, but ultimately this "self" is revealed as a hallucination of perception—an illusion placed on top of the contingent parts of our existence. Consider the body, for instance. The body is said to be approximately 90 percent water. This water is made up of hydrogen and oxygen atoms. Atoms, comprised of energy, are essentially empty space. Where then is the solid entity we depend on and call the body? Science points out that what we call matter and energy are both inseparable and interchangeable. And so the concept of "matter-energy" has arisen, as we attempt through language to convey the constant flow and flux of our universe, and the intricate relationship between all things. Our bodies, as well as every object around them, have never been static and self-contained entities, separate from the changing conditions that create them.

The first year that I was back in this country from India, I met someone who was talking about physical immortality and asserting that medical science might in the future make this a real possibility. Having just returned from India, where death is not so hidden as it is in the West, it seemed clear to me that this was impossible—that death is inexorably linked with birth. We may like to think that science will make it possible for us to be able to control everything, that we will be able to wake up one day, look in the mirror, and say, "You're not going to die." But the body, like everything else, is the interdependent play of conditions.

In the same way, whatever arises in the mind does so in relation to the continually changing process of the inseparable body-mind dynamic. Thoughts and feelings do not come at our invitation. We may create the conditions for the arising of certain mind-states, such as lovingkindness, but it is not a question of absolute determination. We will never be able to successfully declare, "From this point on I will be entirely loving and compassionate." If we create the conditions for change, change will eventually happen; if we create the conditions for radical change, radical change will eventually happen, but not because we simply decide that it will be so, saying, "I am now and forever filled with loving-kindness."

When we understand that there is no being within us who is controlling things, we can see that a state of mind is just that—a state of the mind. It is not *my* state of mind; I did not choose it. Think about how many different mind-states you might have experienced just today. There may have been moments of joy and doubt and hope and fear. Which one is the real you? Any state—of body, mind, or feelings—arises as certain conditions come together, and then vanishes as the conditions pass. Even major diseases of the body such as cancer, or states of mind such as depression, which may seem so solid and enduring, can be recognized as the combination of a multiplicity of arisings. We may be able to discern the mental states or environmental factors that contribute to these conditions, and we may be able to change some of these in order to facilitate our healing, but no amount of willful determination is going to allow us ultimate control over them.

The basis of the Buddha's psychological teaching is that, given the truth of inherent insubstantiality and interdependence, trying to control that which cannot be controlled will never give us the security we all wish for. It will not give us happiness. When we let go of trying to control, when we instead fully connect with our experiences, then we can be drawn through the transparency of all things and arrive at our fundamental interconnectedness.

In this way, understanding anatta, selflessness, allows us to enter a state of equanimity that is like vast space: rich and vivid and dynamic. It contains everything; it does not struggle with anything; it clings to nothing. Looking at others with this kind of equanimity allows us to love everyone as ourselves.

Paul Valéry, the French poet and philosopher, said, "God made everything out of nothing, but the nothing shows through." This nothing is not a bleak vacuity but rather a radiance, a translucence. Dipa Ma was an example of that transparency, having so deeply understood selflessness, and she was the most full and loving person that I could ever imagine. For in her, selflessness had developed into great equanimity. The nothingness showed through brilliantly in Dipa Ma; it shone through her in the love she exhibited for all beings, without exception.

The Bridge of Empathy

CONTEMPORARY PSYCHOLOGICAL RESEARCH shows that some individuals, when they are in a highly agitated state of mind, are oblivious to how they are feeling. Their hearts may be racing, their blood pressure climbing, and they may be sweating profusely, yet they are not aware of being angry or afraid or anxious. About one person in six exhibits this pattern. Being so unaware of their own pain, is it possible that they could understand or empathize with what someone else may be feeling? Being unable to empathize, how can they live complete lives?

When we practice mindfulness, one of the qualities that we are developing is empathy. As we open to the full range of experiences within ourselves, we become aware of what we perceive in each moment, no longer denying some feelings while clinging to others. By coming to know our own pain, we build a bridge to the pain of others, which enables us to step out of our self-absorption and offer help. And when we actually understand how it feels to suffer—in ourselves and in others—we are compelled to live in a way that creates as little harm as possible.

With empathy acting as a bridge to those around us, a true morality arises within. Knowing that someone will suffer if we perform a harmful action or say a hurtful word, we find we do these things less and less. It is a very simple, natural, and heart-full response. Rather than seeing morality as a set of rules, we find a morality that is an uncontrived reluctance to cause suffering.

In Buddhist teachings an image is used to reflect this quality of mind: a feather, held near a flame, instantly curls away from the heat. When our minds become imbued with an understanding of how suffering feels and fill with a compassionate urge not to cause more of it, we naturally recoil from causing harm. This happens without self-consciousness or self-righteousness; it happens as a natural expression of the heart. As Hannah Arendt said, "Conscience is the one who greets you if and when you ever come home."

Two qualities are traditionally attributed to this beautiful and delicate sense of conscience that gives rise to harmlessness: in Pali they are known as *hiri* and *ottapah*, traditionally translated as "moral shame" and "moral dread." The translation is somewhat misleading, as these qualities have nothing to do with fear or shame in the self-deprecating sense. Rather, they have to do with that natural and complete turning away from causing harm. Ottapah, or moral dread, comes from a feeling of disquietude at the possibility of hurting ourselves or others. Hiri, moral shame, manifests in the form of a reluctance to cause pain in others because we know fully in ourselves how that feels.

In this sense, opening to our own suffering can be the source of our deep connection to others. We open to this pain, not for the sake of getting depressed, but for what it has to teach us: seeing things in a different way, having the courage not to harm, recognizing that we are not alone and could never be alone.

Sometimes we are afraid to open to something painful because it seems as though it will consume us. Yet the nature of mindfulness is that it is never overcome by whatever is the present object of awareness. If we are mindful of a twisted or distorted state of mind, the mindfulness is not twisted or distorted. Even the most painful state of mind or the most difficult feeling in the body does not ruin mindfulness. A true opening, born of mindfulness, is marked by spaciousness and grace.

In our culture we are taught to push away, to avoid our feelings. This kind of aversion is the action of a mind caught in separation. Whether in the active, fiery form of anger and rage, or in a more inward, frozen form like fear, the primary function of these mental states is to separate us from what we are experiencing. But the only way that we can be free from suffering ourselves and avoid doing harm to others is by connection—a connection to our own pain and, through awareness and compassion, a connection to the pain of others. We learn not to create separation from anything or anyone. This is empathy.

No Pizza in Nirvana

THE FUNDAMENTAL PURPOSE of meditation is perfect liberation, or nirvana. Nirvana is not our normal conditioned state, in which we seem to be the isolated perceiver of objects "out there" that are constantly arising and passing away. The inner experience of nirvana is incomprehensible and inexpressible, and so the words traditionally used to describe it are phrased in the negative: "unborn," "uncreated," "unconditioned." Once I contemplated writing a book on nirvana, and a friend teased me, "So, you're going to try to 'eff' the ineffable!" Even though it may seem impossible to talk about, nirvana is not impossible to attain, and so we attempt to describe it.

In speaking of nirvana, the Buddha said, "O monks, there is the unborn and the unconditioned. Here the four elements of earth, air, water, and fire have no place. The notions of length and breadth, the subtle and the gross, good and evil, name and form, are altogether destroyed. Neither this world nor the other, no coming, going, or standing, neither death nor birth, nor sense objects are to be found here." Literally, *nirvana* means "blown out," like a candle. Experiencing nirvana means our separateness and suffering are "blown out."

Nirvana is not a state that is known through the senses. As long as there is a subject that is knowing and an object being known, there is change and conditionality. Nirvana is changeless. It cannot pass away because it never began. It is not really an "experience" in the way we commonly use that word.

The peace and the bliss to be found in nirvana are completely distinct and separate from the more familiar kind of

happiness we seek through the senses. The happiness discovered in nirvana is independent of any object we might
experience or any thought we might think. Because of our
conditioning in this materialistic culture, it may be hard to
imagine a kind of happiness that arises free from a particular
experience or sensation.

My teacher Munindra was fond of saying, "There's no
pizza in nirvana; are you still interested in it?" It's a good
question. In our society we are taught to want this and want
that. But no matter what we get, it is never enough because
it doesn't last. So the search for new conditions goes on and
on. We look for new intellectual experiences, new sexual
experiences, and new spiritual experiences. People are even
willing to destroy their bodies, their minds, and their relationships with those they love—destroy their lives—all for
some experience.

Even if something pleasant could endure, we could not
bear for it to go on and on. Who could watch the same
movie over and over without wanting a break? Who could
listen to a sweet sound that never stops? Yet when we seek
rest from one experience, we do so, ironically, by seeking
another. The Buddha taught that the only rest from this
constant tedium and pressure of change is nirvana.

For many of us, the thought of wishing to be "blown
out," to enter into something described only in the negative, or to realize the "unborn" is not necessarily very com-
forting. From the point of view that happiness arises from
new and increasing sensation, nirvana can seem like a secret
death, something terrible, a great chilling void. We might
then believe that the point of spiritual practice is to take
hold of this self—the self that has been with us all our lives,
taking care of us, showing us a good time, being good to
us—and kill it!

This notion of annihilation is a pretty scary prospect, but it has nothing to do with nirvana. One of the things I have always particularly appreciated about the Buddha's teaching is that he did not talk about the self as something lurking within us, needing to be killed, obliterated, or driven out. What he talked about was this: there is no self to begin with, and there never has been. The teachings do not convey the sense that there is something precious inside of us that we're going to lose, nor the sense that there is something awful inside of us that we have to wrestle to the ground and destroy. Our practice, rather than being about killing the ego, is about simply discovering our true nature.

Nirvana is a leap into the unknown, into that which is beyond our conditioned reality, beyond our normal words, beyond our conventional desires and ideas of who we are. When I was first building my house, an architect said, "You can best design the house by looking at the piece of land and experiencing it as incomplete. Then understand that the house will complete it." In that same way, somewhere within each one of us there is a sense that the "terrain" of our lives is incomplete. Because it is an uncomfortable feeling, we might be tempted to condemn it, or to seek ever greater stimulation in order to forget about it. Instead, we might understand this feeling in us as something wonderful that longs for completion, longs for the fulfillment of our lives in that which is beyond ordinary, fleeting happiness, beyond our seemingly separate self.

In meditation we perceive the essencelessness and impermanence of everything in existence—and we acutely feel the insecurity of this. We also know great elation and awe at the wondrousness of this existence, seeing truly what a miracle it is. Having experienced both the elation and the insecurity, the mind settles into a state of equanimity and poise.

In this state of perfect balance there is no leaning forward in anticipation of a future, no grasping, not the slightest impulse toward something "else." There is just *being*. It is here that the silent, wordless opening of nirvana comes about.

The realization of nirvana isn't a fantasy or an arcane achievement we distantly admire because the Buddha accomplished it in a faraway place long ago. It is ours to realize as well. The very fact that the Buddha was a human being points to the possibility for all of us to be free. This opportunity underlies every moment of our lives.

Practicing for Dying

I ANTICIPATED my first trip to Burma with great excitement. Many of my teachers had been from Burma or had done their meditation training there, and I was going to study with their teachers. It felt as if I were going home, as I would experience more fully the lineage of teaching that I was now a part of.

This was the early 1970s, however, and travel to Burma was quite restricted. The visa application process was formidable, and the longest amount of time any tourist was allowed to stay was seven days. Eventually I would learn to prolong the length of my stay by doing what others who were interested in meditating in Burma did: entering from one country, like India, and after seven days leaving for a different country, like Thailand or Nepal, only to apply for another seven-day visa to reenter Burma. Some meditators did this over and over again. It was an expensive and troublesome process, but it allowed us access to that isolated land and its wonderful teachers.

So, with a good deal of effort, money, and planning, I entered Burma for the first time. With high anticipation and many expectations, I arrived in the city of Rangoon and went to the meditation center where my first meditation teacher, S. N. Goenka, had studied. I began my precious seven days of practice, but very soon I developed a terrible cough. It was so persistent that in order to ease my bouts of coughing, I tried to sleep sitting up. I was miserable. I felt bitter and fretful. I kept thinking, "I spent all this money to come here to be with these special teachers in this magical place, and now it's all ruined because I got sick. I can't practice well, I feel awful, and I can't stop coughing."

I finally said this, in a complaining, self-pitying voice, to Sayama, the woman who was the main teacher at the retreat center. She looked at me quietly for a moment, and then she said, "Well, I guess this will be good practice for when you die."

I was dumbfounded. After all, I was a member of a very groovy generation, dedicated to looking for pleasant altered states of consciousness and amazing experiences. Like most spiritual seekers I knew, I fully intended to die consciously. I imagined I would be lying in bed, surrounded by my friends reading aloud to me from *The Tibetan Book of the Dead*. There would be candles and incense and lovely music. But somehow that image of my conscious death had not included the possibility of any physical discomfort! I would be dying, but I was going to feel fine!

It was shocking to realize that Sayama was absolutely right. The distressing experience of sickness I was having then was an opportunity to practice for the time when my body would be malfunctioning in death. I realized how limited my sense of spirituality was—as though mindfulness was to be applied only to the "good" times, as though awareness had to crumble in the face of sickness, pain, and disappointment. I had, in fact, drawn a boundary around my experiences, saying in effect, "Anything that falls outside of this boundary, anything I don't like, should not be a part of my reality. So I just won't pay attention to it; whether it comes up in life or while on the meditation cushion, I won't accept it." Those words still echo in my mind, and they sound just like the voice of a querulous four-year-old.

Death is not necessarily a pleasant experience, and in fact, many of our life experiences are not pleasant. But, these experiences are some of the most fruitful opportunities for real spiritual practice—practice that prepares us for all of life's truths. If we have the ability to remain balanced in the face of unpleasantness, if we can remain mindful when we are miserable, then every moment, including our last ones, may be filled with the peace that we yearn for. So today, if I am ill or in pain, I remember Sayama saying: "Well, I guess this will be good practice for when you die."

The Transparent World

THE BUDDHA TAUGHT that everything exists in dependence on conditions, in a relationship that is continually changing and, thus, essentially insubstantial. In the same way that the objects of our experience are subject to change, so too are our ways of thinking, our conceptual frameworks. We may talk about the Empire State Building as being very tall, until we compare it to the World Trade Center, which is taller. We might search for an object that is inherently tall, but we will fail to find it, because all of our ways of comprehending exist in relationship to something else.

The insubstantiality of our ways of thinking, our concepts, is revealed to us over and over. It was once revealed to
me in a powerful way when I visited the Lama Foundation, a
spiritual community in New Mexico. In May 1996, flames
swept across northern New Mexico, destroying seventy-five
hundred acres of forest as well as thirty-two homes and
structures in the Lama community. The residents of Lama
Foundation were forced to evacuate. When they were allowed to return, they discovered that the once richly for-
ested mountain had been transformed into a desert of ash,
rubble, and dead or dying trees.

Our drive up to the foundation land brought us through
an eerie scene. The landscape was utterly transformed; it
was strangely like entering the negative of a photo, the sky-
line filled with silhouettes of charred trees. As we tried to
orient ourselves, we spotted familiar places now completely
devastated.

As I spoke with the people who lived on the mountain,
they talked about how they'd always identified themselves
as part of that community, part of the Lama Foundation.
They were now forced to ask themselves: "Where is the
Lama Foundation? Is it in the land and therefore largely
destroyed? In the present community and therefore largely
intact? In the spirit, which can be found in many different
places, wherever people do spiritual practice? Is it located
in the experiences that countless people have had over the
years when they have visited, and so existent wherever they
are? Is it in the effect that all of those people have had on
others, and therefore spread throughout the world? Can we
find the one thing that is the Lama Foundation?"

When fixed notions of designations and categories are
dissolved, we see that we live in an intricate, extraordinary
world of change, all mutable, boundless, and transitory. We

live in a world of transparency, of insubstantiality. Experiences do not exist as a substantial reality apart from the conditions that created them.

In relating to our life, we have a fundamental choice: we can be cognizant of and accepting of this ephemeral, fleeting world, or we can cling to a mistaken notion of solidity, of inherently permanent categories. But if we deny the insubstantiality of things, we miss the living, flowing nature of the universe. We become trapped in the limitations of mere concepts and don't realize how constricted we are until we let go. We let go of a singular self-identity and find the understanding of where Lama was not destroyed, and where we do not die. Without a solid, unyielding, rigid view, we discover the expansiveness of life, its extraordinary richness of possibility. Then, no matter what the experience, we can know it with a heart that is unbound.

Chili Peppers

ONCE, on a meditation retreat in Burma, I was calmly eating lunch when I unexpectedly bit down on a whole chili pepper. My mouth caught on fire, and so did my mind. "I've got to get out of this country," I immediately thought to myself. "This spicy food is going to make me sick. I'm going to get an ulcer."

I had an interview scheduled with my teacher, Sayadaw U Pandita, right after lunch. When I went in to see him, I asked as casually as I could, "Why is it that Burmese people like the taste of chilies so much?" He said to me, "We don't like the taste of chilies very much." Indignantly I asked, "Why do you put so many in the food then?" He replied,

"We have a belief that the stinging, burning sensation you get when you bite down on a chili pepper will clear your palate, and that clearing your palate is very good for your digestion. We believe chili peppers are good for your health, and we put a lot of them in the food." So, it turned out that the same burning sensation that made me worry about stomach ulcers, the Burmese thought of as being good for one's health. The same sensation, two very different reactions.

One of the most powerful moments of insight we can have is when, in the midst of an experience, we see that there is a clear difference between our immediate sensation and the mental response we add to it. We then start to see that what we consider our experience of reality has two essentially different aspects.

The first aspect has to do with the natural property of any experience and is universal. If you bite down on a chili pepper, and your taste buds are functioning, no matter who you are or where you live, you will experience burning. The first aspect is that which is true by nature—the direct, unembellished, unelaborated truth of the moment.

The second aspect has to do with our concepts—the interpretations we add to the direct experience. These are based on our desires, memories, belief systems, past experiences, and fears. The full force of our psychological, personal, and cultural conditioning comes to bear in that moment. We embellish the experience and draw conclusions about what it means for our own lives.

The practice of mindfulness allows us to discern these two distinct aspects. Through mindfulness we can see that the interpretations, the feelings about what has arisen, the ideas about it, are not an inherent part of that particular experience. Not that we would want to, or ever could, eradicate the aspect of reality that is conceptual and interpretive. However, having an intimate awareness of both these parts makes us aware of the sea of concepts that we usually drown ourselves in.

When we understand that a particular experience does not mandate a particular interpretation, we awaken to what is called in Buddhist teaching "karmic vision." There are so many ways of perceiving and interpreting and feeling about the very same event, depending on all of the conditioning we bring to that moment. As Kalu Rinpoche explained, "If a hundred people sleep and dream, each of them will experience a different world in their dream. Everyone's dream might be said to be true, but it would be meaningless to ascertain that only one person's dream was the true world and all others were fallacies. There's truth for each perceiver, according to the karmic patterns conditioning their perceptions."

The world that is created by our karmic vision is rich and varied. Being mindful, we can remember how much our own worldview affects what we make of each experience, and how the same experience might be interpreted very differently by another.

Joseph Goldstein and I were once staying in a hotel in London when, in the middle of the night, the fire alarm began blaring. I bolted out of bed, thinking, "What should I do?" We were on the sixth floor, and I had recently sprained my ankle. I knew it was dangerous to take the elevator, so I would have to make it down the stairs. "What should I take with me?" I wondered. The alarm kept blaring, so I just grabbed my passport and left the room. In the corridor, I met up with Joseph, who was staying in the next room. He had taken his passport and his notes for the Dharma talks he would be giving during the next retreat.

We arrived downstairs to find the lobby filled with people. It was an amazing scene. Some people seemed to have
packed everything they owned and carried it down the
stairs. Others had taken nothing. There were women wearing white gloves, pearls, and makeup; some men were in
three-piece suits, and others were literally half undressed.
And as I stood there, at 3:00 A.M., the thought occurred to
me, "This is how life actually is all the time, with all of us
responding to an experience in our own unique ways."

Each person's view of events is conditioned by so many
things, but when we become afraid or uncertain, we tend to
cling to our perceptions as if they were universally true. We
confuse the direct nature of an experience with our particular reaction, as though that reaction were mandated by the
experience itself. Thus the world suddenly becomes very
small. This is called fixation. When we imagine that all
other people are perceiving the world just as we are, or that
they should be, we not only reinforce our subjective perceptions but also lose the capacity to connect intimately with
others, and we deny the richness of their experiences.

By coming to know the difference between the natural
property of any experience and our interpretation of it, we
begin to realize how immensely relative our reactions are.
Recognizing that an incredible array of feelings and interpretations and thoughts can arise in response to any event,
we see that we do not need to cling so ferociously to our
own reactions. We need not feel trapped by the world we
find in each moment, once we realize how intricately it is
shaped by our perceptions.

Knowing the Deathless

THE BUDDHA, shocked upon seeing a corpse for the first time and realizing that the same fate awaited him, left his home to seek freedom from the cycle of life and death. "I who am subject to change," he said, "should not seek refuge in that which is also subject to change." Throughout the ages there has been spiritual longing for that which is untouched by change or death—a true peace. The Buddha himself said, "The spiritual faculties reach to the Deathless, merge in the Deathless, and end in the Deathless."

My mother died when I was nine years old. When I was eighteen, I went to India in search of that which would not die. I think death meant abandonment to me; it was something both to run away from and to resent. I was looking for a refuge in life and hoped meditation practice would reveal it to me.

Many of us may try to hold onto life as our sanctuary from death—that is, until we see clearly what life itself is. There is nothing we can have that we cannot also lose. There is nothing that is born that will not also die. Our lives are made up, as Emerson put it, of "the vanishing volatile froth of the present which any shadow will alter, any thought blow away, any event annihilate."

A Buddhist text says it this way:

> Know all things to be like this—a mirage, a cloud castle, a dream, an apparition, without essence but with qualities that can be seen. Know all things to be like this—as the moon in a bright sky in some clear lake reflected, though to that lake the moon has never moved. Know all things to be like this—as an echo that derives from music, sounds, and weeping, yet in that echo is no melody.

> Know all things to be like this—as a magician makes illusions of horses, oxen, carts, and other things, nothing is as it appears.

The question then becomes: "Is there anything in life that resembles a solid, separate self that one day dies? Is there anything permanent? What are we able to hold on to anyway?" When we open our awareness to ask these questions, we come to see clearly the nature of our existence. In asking "Who is it that dies?" we get the first glimmer of what the deathless might be.

Looking carefully, we see that the separate self we have cherished and fought for and wept over is merely an assumed identity. All of our conceptualizations and desires and fears have been born from the fabricated tyranny of something that never existed in the first place. When we unmask the illusion of the separate self, a direct knowledge of the transparency and complete interdependence of all of life is revealed to us. When we realize that there has never been a separate self that dies, we recognize that the Deathless is not "other," and we are freed by the truth of this realization: death is not separate from life.

Compassion Is a Verb

As Thich Nhat Hanh, the Vietnamese Zen monk, points out, "Compassion is a verb." It is not a thought or a sentimental feeling but is rather a movement of the heart. As classically defined in Pali, compassion is "the trembling or the quivering of the heart." But how do we get our hearts to do that? How do we "do" compassion?

Compassion is born out of lovingkindness. It is born of

knowing our oneness, not just thinking about it or wishing it were so. It is born out of the wisdom of seeing things exactly as they are. But compassion also arises from the practice of inclining the mind, of refining our intention. The Dalai Lama once said, "I don't know why people like me so much. It must be because I try to be compassionate, to have *bodhicitta*, the aspiration of compassion." He doesn't claim success—he claims a commitment to really trying.

Is there a difference, in quality or quantity, between the compassion any of us might feel and the compassion of the Dalai Lama? Is it that he experiences more compassionate moments in a row? Or is the actual quality of compassion different? While this can be seen from many different perspectives, one traditional view would say that a moment of compassion any one of us feels is as pure, as deep, as direct as anyone else's; but what happens is that we may lose touch with it more often. We get distracted, we forget, we get caught up in something else, or we confuse another feeling for the state of compassion.

We might at times think that we are feeling compassion when in fact what we are feeling is fear. We may be afraid to take an action, to confront a person or a situation, to be forceful or to reach out. Under the guise of believing we are being kind and compassionate, we hold back. From the Buddhist perspective, this lack of effort to ease our own or another's suffering is seen as lack of courage. Because it is not easy to see lack of courage in oneself, we prefer to think we are being compassionate rather than afraid.

Another state of mind that is often confused with compassion is guilt. When we see someone who is suffering while we are fairly happy, or if we are happy in a way that another person is not, we might inwardly feel that we do not deserve our happiness, or that we should hold back our happiness out of pity for the other. But guilt, in Buddhist psychology, is defined as a type of self-hatred and a form of anger.

Certainly there are times when we recognize that we have acted unskillfully, and we feel concern and remorse. This kind of remorse can be important and healing. This is in contrast to the guilt we feel as a state of contraction, in which we endlessly review what we might have done or said in the past. In this state of guilt we become center stage; rather than acting to serve others, we act to get rid of the guilt and thus only serve ourselves. Guilt drains our energy, whereas compassion gives us the strength to reach out to help others.

In order to let go of the feelings of fear and guilt, and move into true compassion, we need to see without hesitation whatever we may be feeling or doing. One of the virtues of awareness is that we can simply look without judgment at what we are actually experiencing. Not being afraid of our fear or guilt, we can say, "Oh, yes, that's fear, that's guilt; that's what's happening right now." And then we can reestablish our intention to be compassionate.

When we practice compassion, we may make the mistake of trying to lay a veneer of caring on top of whatever we are actually feeling: "I mustn't feel fear, I mustn't feel guilt, I must only feel compassion, because that is my dedication." It is important to remember, though, that the clarity at the heart of compassion comes from wisdom. We don't have to struggle to be someone we are not, hating ourselves for our confused feelings. Seeing clearly what is happening is the ground out of which compassion will arise.

What is most important is the mind's unshakable intention to see through to the root of suffering. We need strength, courage, and wisdom to be able to open so deeply. And then the compassion can come forth.

The state of compassion is whole and sustaining; the compassionate mind is not broken or shattered by facing states of suffering. It is spacious and resilient. Compassion is nourished by the wisdom of our interconnectedness. This understanding transcends a martyrdom in which we habitually think only of others, never caring about ourselves. And it transcends a self-centered caring in which we have concern only about ourselves and never bother about others. Wisdom of our interconnectedness arises hand in hand with learning to truly love ourselves. The Buddha said that if we truly loved ourselves, we would never harm another. For in harming another, we diminish who we are. When we can love ourselves, we give up the idea that we do not deserve the love and attention we are theoretically willing to give to others.

By bringing awareness to the truth of the present moment, and also holding a vision of our heart's deepest wish to be loving toward all, we establish our dedication to compassion. Perhaps the shining manifestation of compassion in the Dalai Lama is a reflection not only of the number of moments he is compassionate, or of how these moments transform the quality of his presence, but also a reflection of his complete confidence in the possibility and importance of being a truly loving person.

Part Three

Living with Wisdom and Compassion

THROUGHOUT HISTORY there have been individuals who have realized the truth, individuals who radiate a sense of wholeness born of clear seeing and love. When we hear about such seemingly extraordinary people, or if we are fortunate enough to meet one of them, we see in them the latent capacity that is within each of us; we remember our true selves. Meditation practice brings our latent wisdom and compassion to life. Once developed through practice, these qualities give rise to the uncontrived desire to help others. The knowledge of our interconnectedness with all beings, and the actions that naturally flow from it, also continually return us to our true selves, engendering empowerment, gratefulness, and deep awareness. This spiritual power manifests in our own lives, in our own everyday world. Living the practice through heartfelt action and understanding arises naturally out of dedication to one's own liberation and to the liberation of all beings. In reality, we can live with a heart as wide as the world.

The Buddha's Revolution

WHEN THE Buddha taught 2,500 years ago, the so-
cial structure in India was built on a rigid philosophical system. According to the view of the world that prevailed at
that time, everything belonged to a category that had a spe-
cific nature and a corresponding duty, or purpose, in life.
For example, it was seen as the nature or duty of fire to burn
and of rocks to be hard, of grass to grow and be green, and
of cows to eat grass and produce milk. The responsibility of
every being was to realize its own nature and to conform to
an ideal disposition particular to them. This disposition was
considered immutable truth.

Socially, this concept came to be translated into the caste
system. People were born destined to fulfill a certain nature.
It was the duty of certain classes or castes of people to rule,
of Brahmans to mediate with divine forces, and of certain
other people to be engaged in production of food and material goods. Within this worldview, actions conceived of as
moral and appropriate for one caste or gender were felt to
be completely immoral for another. It was proper and bene-
ficial for a male member of the Brahman caste to read and
study the scriptures, for example, while this was absolutely
forbidden and considered abhorrent for someone who was
an outcast.

Into this social context, the Buddha introduced his revolutionary teachings. What he taught in terms of ethics was
radical then, and it is radical today. He stated that what
determines whether an action is moral or immoral is the
volition of the person performing it, the intention that gives
rise to it. "Not by birth is one a Brahman, or an outcast,"

the Buddha said, "but by deeds." This teaching, in effect, declared the entire social structure of India—considered sacrosanct by many—to be of no spiritual significance at all.

The Buddha was stating that the only status that truly matters is the status of personal goodness, and personal goodness is attained through personal effort, not by birth. It did not matter if you were a man or a woman, wealthy or poor, a Brahman or an outcast—an action based on greed would have a certain kind of result, and an action based on love would have another kind of result. "A true Brahman is one who is gentle, who is wise and caring," he said, thus completely negating the importance of caste, skin color, class, and gender in any consideration of morality.

The Buddha was clearly saying that we are not held to different standards. The truth of suffering and the end of suffering, tied so intimately to our ethical behavior, is the same for all of us. No matter who is acting, the intention or volition behind the action is the karmic seed that is planted. The motivating force behind the action is thus considered the most important and potent aspect of the action. Essentially, our intentions are an expression of the power of our minds. Transforming our motivations transforms our whole life: our happiness, our degree of connection with others, our freedom. None of this is fixed in the particular externals of who we are; it is all held in the universal potential of what we might become.

By denying that spiritual authority and capacity were invested in one particular class of people, the Buddha was acknowledging that we do not need someone else to mediate with the divine, we don't need a special class whose duty it is to delve deeply into spirituality. It is in everyone's capacity to be spiritual; it is everyone's duty, everyone's role. We can all utilize the power of awareness for our own liberation; our truth is a "self-witnessed" truth, our faith tested and tried by our own experience. The most powerful work is first done within the mind, because the mind is the fore-runner of all elements of life. By pointing out to us the crucial importance of our intentions, the Buddha was mak-ing clear that each of us is responsible for our own mind, and therefore for our own freedom. It was a commonly held view in ancient India that sexual desire arising in a man's mind was a woman's fault, being the result of the female's temptation of the male. (Doesn't this sound familiar, even today?) The Buddha refuted this view by saying that, what-ever the object, the nature of desire arising in anyone's mind is the same, and the choice of how to respond is the responsibility of the person in whose mind the desire arose. In the end, deflecting responsibility merely condemns us to being a disempowered agent in our own lives. Freedom is a real potential, but how we work with our minds is up to us.

Only we can know our own motivations. In any action, what is seen from the outside is simply the act itself. If I were to hand you a book, anyone witnessing that would see only my hand reaching and offering the book to you. I may be giving it to you because I like you and want you to have the book; I may be giving it to you because I know you have a book I want and I hope that you will see fit to offer it in exchange; I may be giving the book to you because we are in a room full of people and I want to appear to be a gener-ous person; or I may be acting from a host of other motiva-tions. The difference is that in one instance my motivation would be cultivating generosity, in another, greed. Given the emphasis that the teachings place on the liberating value of transforming one's intentions, it is critical that we know what our own intentions are. For in our intention lies the power of our minds, and the possibility of essential change.

In this single teaching on the power of intention the Buddha burst the bubble of social class: the deflecting of responsibility, the mindless deference to religious authority, and the defining of potential according to external criteria. In this one teaching he returned the potential for freedom back to each one of us.

Caught Up

TWO OF MY FRIENDS once worked together for some time, and then had a falling out. They did not speak to each other for a year—until circumstances threw them together again for just a few minutes. Though it was a brief time, they had a genuine reconciliation. A short while after that, one of them suddenly became very ill. As we awaited a diagnosis, I called the other friend. After commenting on how we never know what will happen, she reflected gratefully on their renewed connection. "I'm so glad we had that moment together," she said. Then recalling another situation in which she had recently cleaned the slate from a past personal conflict, she said happily, "I'm pretty caught up!" I loved that comment. Since we do not, in fact, know what will happen to any of us at any time, there is tremendous relief in being "pretty caught up," rather than trailing a legacy of resentments, annoyances, and feelings left unspoken.

Based in part on the knowledge that we never actually know if we will meet again, Asian monastic communities have a formalized ritual of forgiveness when saying goodbye. When U Pandita first came to teach at the Insight Meditation Society, it was the first time that he had worked entirely with Westerners. It was a very intense course of practice. While many of us found great personal benefit in working with him, there were also some cultural misunderstandings. When U Pandita prepared to leave IMS, as part of the closing ceremony of the retreat he said, "If I have hurt or harmed you in any way, either intentionally or unintentionally, I ask your forgiveness. And if you have hurt me in any way, intentionally or unintentionally, I forgive you." In this way he could leave without carrying fixed definitions of anyone based on the past. No one would be pegged in his mind as "the one who said that inappropriate thing" or "the one who wouldn't follow any guidance." And he could be freed of any resentment or bad feelings anyone might hold toward him. He did this not because things had been so very bad during the retreat but because it is considered the proper way of saying good-bye. It reflects the importance of letting go of past experiences so that we do not carry around codified impressions of each other.

In fact, when I next met U Pandita, about six months later, I felt very different, and he seemed different to me. Even though our previous relationship had been quite good, it felt as if our relationship were beginning again, and the freshness of a new beginning was wonderful. Because he had performed that ritual six months before, we were able to look at each other free from our previous experiences, good or bad. This kind of forgiveness creates the possibility of meeting someone we know after a separation, and both coming together with open hearts. And if we do not meet again, we will be free of any lingering entanglements. We will be "caught up."

Bearing a grudge may feel like a kind of security: "I know who I am. I am the one who was hurt by that certain person and will always be angry at him." But that feeling of security is false; it does not include the sure knowledge of our own and the other person's death. When death steps in, we suffer with bitter regret over things that will remain forever left unsaid and feelings that won't be communicated. The time for catching up is now. There is not enough time later, or any certainty about what the future holds. Any other vision of reality is constructed by the mind as it refuses to believe that we must someday die.

Every good-bye that we say in our lives is truly a letting go into the unknown. And so, in every parting there is a chance to get caught up, to liberate ourselves of negative mind-states, and to offer this liberation to others.

The Mistake

A FEW YEARS AGO, in Tucson, Arizona, the Dalai Lama gave a week-long series of teachings on patience. Over twelve hundred people attended the event. We all stayed in a resort hotel outside of town, transforming what was a commercial venue into something of a retreat center. Every morning and afternoon, the Dalai Lama would teach, and in the evenings, we Western Buddhist teachers would speak on a particular aspect of patience. Sylvia Boorstein and I were the first Western teachers scheduled to speak. I must admit to feeling a little anxiety in talking to such a large audience, and I wanted to be sure to get it "right." Fortunately, a few nights later, the Dalai Lama, in his wonderful way, gave us all a profound teaching about what "getting it right" is truly about.

He was explicating a chapter of Shantideva's *Guide to the Bodhisattva's Way of Life*, an eighth-century text covering the entire path to enlightenment. Moving line by line through the manuscript, the Dalai Lama presented his commentary in Tibetan, and while it was being translated, he examined the upcoming lines he would speak on next. The Dalai Lama's English is quite good, and at one point during a translation, he looked up from the manuscript and said to the translator, "You're mistaken. That's not what I said." The disagreement that followed was about a matter of syntax—whether Shantideva, in establishing a point about patience, had said, "She said that to him" or "He said that to her." The translator responded by saying, "No, Your Holiness, I did not make a mistake. In fact the text says 'He said that to her.' " The Dalai Lama replied, "No, it says, 'She said that to him.' "

The translator again disagreed, and they discussed it back and forth for a while: "He said that to her"; "No, 'She said that to him' "; and so on. The Dalai Lama then turned back the pages of the text until he got to the disputed section. He looked at it, then burst into loud laughter, saying mirthfully, "Hah, hah, hah! Oh, I made a mistake."

There he was, having been caught in an error in front of twelve hundred people, laughing uproariously about it. I doubt that I would have been laughing so freely had I made a mistake when addressing those twelve hundred people a few nights before. He was a wonderful role model of a non-constricted heart, of the natural ebullience that comes when we are not defending a concept we have of who we are.

When we try to project a certain image, or be someone special, or be perfect and never make a mistake, there is a tightening in the heart. When we relax the heart, not trying to "be" someone special, we can be who we really are, with honesty, with perspective, and with compassion. These qualities are the conditions of liberation, whatever is happening. And when we are truly free, we might, like the Dalai Lama, be able to laugh loudly when we make a mistake.

Greedy, Grumpy, Sleepy, Anxious, and/or Dubious

THERE WAS A WOMAN who left her apartment one morning to go to work. She walked to the street and took out the keys to unlock her car. Just as she was putting the key in the door lock, she noticed that her car seemed lower to the ground than usual. When she looked down, she was shocked to see that all four of her tires had been stolen! Her immediate response was to march off to the nearest shopping center and buy herself a pair of silk pajamas as a way to comfort herself. Only then could she go back home and call the police.

My friend Sylvia Boorstein, who is also a meditation teacher, uses this story as a way of describing the Five Hindrances. In the classical Buddhist teachings, the five hindrances are desire, aversion, sloth, restlessness, and doubt. They are typically used to describe the states of mind that distract us in meditation practice, but they also are mental states that hinder us from being mindful of what is happening in any moment. Being lost in one of these mental states, our sense of what is possible is restricted. Our minds cannot operate in an open and free way. Furthermore, each of us has a tendency to respond to circumstances in predominantly one or another of these modes.

In the story of the stolen tires, the person's reaction to the situation is a perfect example of the state of mind of someone lost in the hindrance of desire. Now, imagine someone who has a stronger tendency toward anger than to desire. This person goes downstairs, starts to put the car key in the door lock, and the same thing happens—she discovers her tires have been stolen. She gets furious and starts hitting the car. She kicks the car and then goes back into the apartment building and starts yelling at the superintendent: "Why haven't you paid more careful attention?" When she goes to work, she is angry and unkind toward people there. After all, it only seems right to her that the difficulty should be spread around.

Next there is the person who tends to be slothful. She goes to her car and discovers that her tires have been stolen. Then she goes back to her apartment, calls in to work, and says, "I just can't cope. I'm too worn out. I'll be in tomorrow." She takes a nap for a few hours, and only then does she feel she has the energy necessary to deal with the situation.

Then there is the person prone to getting lost in the hindrance of restlessness. Because restlessness often manifests as fretfulness and agitation, one aspect of this hindrance is a state of anxiety. When this sort of person discovers that her tires have been stolen, she starts fretting. She thinks to herself, "Today it was the tires; tomorrow it will be the car; then after that, it will be me."

Finally, there is the hindrance of doubt, which manifests in us as "being stuck." When we are lost in doubt, we don't know what to do next. Our energy and awareness collapse. Everything seems fragmented, and the mind spins out of control as it jumps from one thing to another. In this particular circumstance of the stolen tires, the state of mind is likely to be one of self-doubt and self-blame. The woman sees that her tires have been stolen but just stands there, saying to herself, "Why do I always make such poor choices? Why did I park here? Why do I live in such a bad neighborhood? This must be all my fault." Not knowing what to do except blame herself, she feels confused and uncertain, and cannot take any constructive action to improve the situation.

We could call this story "The Tale of Greedy, Grumpy, Sleepy, Anxious, or Dubious." Or, because sometimes we feel that we are struggling with all five of the hindrances at once, it could also be called "The Tale of Greedy, Grumpy, Sleepy, Anxious, *and* Dubious." Yet, however many hindrances arise in the mind, or however intense they may be, we need not judge them or ourselves for their existence. Wisdom, gained through mindfulness, shows us that they are simply passing mind-states. We see them clearly and with a sense of spaciousness. Then we are not bound to act in a particular way, controlled by that mind-state.

So here we are one morning as we go to our car and discover the tires have been stolen. We might feel an urge to go buy silk pajamas, or blame everyone we encounter for our troubles, or take a nap, or have our worries proliferate into deep anxiety, or collapse into uncertainty and doubt. Although one or several of these conditioned tendencies are bound to arise, if we are mindful *of* them instead of being driven *by* them, we will have expansiveness of mind. In this expansiveness, we have the freedom to choose our response to any situation.

The Middle of the Middle Way

THE TEACHINGS of the Buddha are known as the Middle Way, or the Middle Path, because they avoid the extremes of overindulgence in the senses on the one hand, and excessive asceticism and self-mortification on the other. The life of the Buddha before his enlightenment, as it is told, exemplified both of these extremes. When he was still called Prince Siddhartha, the Buddha lived surrounded by the glitter of sensual delights. It is said that his parents were so concerned that he be protected from any unhappiness that they employed a crew of gardeners to work throughout the night in order to pluck out any blossoms that were wilting, so that the prince should not be troubled by the sight of something that was imperfect.

Eventually, when Siddhartha finally witnessed the suffering that does exist in the world, he was compelled to pursue the truth. First he followed a path of self-mortification that lasted for about six years. He lived a life of exceeding renunciation and asceticism. In India at that time, it was believed that by torturing or humiliating the body, one could free the spirit, enabling it to soar beyond the confines of the material world. The Buddha, however, after the many years of his intense asceticism, realized that neither the extreme of indulgence nor the extreme of deprivation led to the goal of true liberation.

The world of indulgence is intoxicating but hollow, and it surrounds us in a fog that keeps us from looking for anything deeper. Meanwhile, when we are intoxicated with the senses, the pain of others threatens the feel-good complacency that accompanies our self-indulgence. Thus we tend to disregard the suffering of others, along with trying to cover up our own inner suffering. And so we end up living isolated from the fullness of life.

Similarly, the path of self-mortification and asceticism only reinforces feelings of self-deprecation and self-hatred, which keep us separate from the love that is at the crux of spiritual transformation. These days we might not be very attracted to becoming ascetics and practicing self-mortification, but we still abuse and humiliate the body in hopes of finding happiness, as seen in the epidemic of eating disorders in our society. Another, perhaps more hidden, form of self-mortification is to create tormented relationships with our own mind, as if the abusive force of self-judgment and self-hatred might somehow liberate us.

Following the Middle Way between these extremes does not mean taking a little indulgence and a little self-mortification and mixing them together. It isn't as if we say to ourselves, "Well, I have spent the last few days in self-indulgence; maybe it's time for some self-mortification. If I spend an equal number of days in each, they'll balance out." Nor is the Middle Way about being mediocre, finding the lowest common denominator of the two extremes of self-indulgence and self-mortification and simply being indolent. Rather, it is about seeing the tension and unhappiness of each extreme and arriving at a completely different place, one that doesn't fall into either category. We are not drawn by these two extremes. The Middle Way is a balance of moral integrity, centered concentration, and clear insight. We find the Middle Way, the place of balance, from a complete revisioning of ourselves, of what we are capable, and of where happiness is to be found. And we come to follow it out of love for ourselves and others, born of the grateful and delighted recognition of our potential to be free and to be of benefit to the world. Understanding where true happiness is to be found, we give ourselves what we need, and we are vigilant about what we don't need.

Walking the Middle Way is a process of continual discovery every moment. We cannot rely on the Buddha's walking of the Middle Way twenty-five hundred years ago, or even our own discovery of it yesterday. Open and vulnerable and alive, we must realize it over and over again in each moment. Out of awareness and compassion for ourselves and others, we uncover the place within us that is the expression of the liberated mind. Thus the Middle Way is both the path to and the manifestation of freedom.

Because of the innumerable times and ways we encounter it in each day, the Middle Way can be seen as being like a fractal, which is an irregular geometric shape that replicates itself in similar forms over a wide range of sizes. In nature, for instance, often a small portion of something appears in reduced scale like a replica of the whole. Coastlines are jagged whether viewed from the immense distance of a satellite, the far distance of an airplane, or standing just above them on the overhanging bluffs. The entire leaf of a fern resembles a magnified version of one of its own smaller parts. Mountains have the same rough, irregular forms whether we see them from a great distance or look at them close up in chunks of granite. Even the vast solar system resembles an enormously magnified atom.

Each and every moment of finding balance between the extremes of self-mortification and indulgence is a perfect replica of the great Middle Way to liberation. Each moment of balance is an articulation of the entire path in its completion. Liberation not only is the goal of the path but is also found in its continually unfolding process. On the Middle Way, we find freedom not just at the end of the journey, but in the middle, and in the middle of the middle, and in the middle of the middle of the middle. Each step on the way to freedom is freedom.

Prayers at the Western Wall

THE Western Wall in Jerusalem, once known as the Wailing Wall, is considered to be one of the most holy sites of the Jewish world. It is part of the retaining wall of a historic temple built in the second century BCE. There is a sacred custom that involves writing a prayer on a piece of paper and placing the paper in a crack somewhere in the Wall. When I was in Jerusalem, I went there to place my prayers in the Wall among the others.

I followed this custom in the spirit of prayer most meaningful to me, that is, without addressing a supreme being or using a tone of beseeching, but rather in the spirit of metta, the practice of lovingkindness. Metta means inclining the heart toward the happiness and safety of all beings and directing the power of our intention in the realization of that aim. So, on my piece of paper, I wrote out my prayers for friends who were sick, friends whose parents were dying, and so on, and put it among all the others in one of the cracks in the Wall.

The next day, when I went back to the Western Wall, I noticed that my piece of paper was still up there, which seemed amazing, considering the hundreds of people who put their prayers in the Wall each day. For some reason, it seemed to me to be a good portent that my paper hadn't fallen out or been knocked to the ground.

I returned the next day to check the Wall again. This time I wasn't quite sure that I could spot my own little yellow piece of paper with wishes for the happiness and well-being of my friends, and I left feeling somewhat disheartened.

When I went back on the fourth day, I was even more upset, because now I definitely couldn't distinguish my particular paper from all of the others. Had it stayed up there or fallen?

On the fifth day, when I went back, still worried about my piece of paper, I knew it was hopeless. The Wall was covered with thousands of other bits of paper, all bearing prayers. I would never know what had happened to mine.

Then suddenly, I realized how unreasonable my fixation with my own particular prayers had been. All at once, it didn't matter whether I could distinguish my prayers from all the others. Each prayer in some way echoed every other prayer. Each one of us who had gone to the Wall had expressed our own version of the universal, primal urge toward happiness, toward peace, for ourselves or for those we love. No matter what the particulars, we were all actually saying the same thing. It no longer mattered whether I was looking at my paper or at the paper of any other person. My wishes were reflected in their prayers and their prayers were reflected in mine.

No matter how we pray or in what language, no matter what religion we practice, if any, no matter what country we come from, all of us fundamentally want the same things: to be happy, to be safe, to be free. That day, standing before the Western Wall, the universal cry of all beings wanting to be happy, including myself, rose up in one voice.

Something and Nothing

"WHY is there something when there could be nothing?" A friend once told me that this is the central question behind Ludwig Wittgenstein's philosophical works. Later, when I was discussing this idea with another friend, she said, "Well, as Buddhist practitioners, we can also ask, 'Why is there nothing when there could be something?'" Indeed, I thought, why is there nothing lasting, nothing substantial, when it seems like there should be *something*? How can this whole world arise, yet there be nothing to hold on to? How can the entire universe appear, only to vanish over time?

Much of our personal suffering is caused by falling into one of two extreme views about reality—that everything is something or that everything is nothing. In one view we feel that there must be something secure or substantial to be found somewhere in the world. There must be something lasting that we can see, hear, smell, taste, touch, or know. Everything then matters a lot, because we have a continual hope that somewhere there is perfect security and unchanging happiness, and we continually seek it, only to be disappointed. When we are caught or lost in this view, we grasp and cling to a world of change and appearance, and we suffer.

In the other extreme view, nothing at all matters. Everything is a kind of void or blank, and we live in random, hopeless chaos. This nihilistic view leads to paralysis. It is the worldview that says, "Since everything is empty and insubstantial, what difference does anything make anyway? Why do anything?" We fall into apathy and disconnection, and we suffer.

The Middle Way of the Buddha avoids both these extreme views. Things are not inherently permanent, nor is emptiness the sole expression of reality. Our lives rest in that very delicate place where everything is arising, and yet it has no substance. Reality is shimmering, translucent, and vital; and yet it's insubstantial, fleeting, and evanescent. It is crucial for us to understand that while everything that arises is insubstantial, it is also consequential. Because it is hard for words to convey this paradox, the Buddha often used images to describe the nature of existence. He said that we experience life like a rainbow, an echo, a dream, like a drop of dew on a blade of grass, like a flash of lightning in a summer sky.

Through insight we come to see both the something and the nothing of existence. We see that anything that can be known with this body or this mind, known through our senses, is fleeting and insubstantial, like a rainbow. We also see that our experience arises and passes in accordance with the laws of nature, such as the law of karma. We see that we do not live in an accidental, random, haphazard universe. There is conditionality in this world, interconnection, and relatedness.

When we perceive the transparency, the insubstantiality of life, we grow in wisdom. When we perceive relatedness within life, the interconnectedness, we grow in love. One never excludes the other. Rather, they are like the two wings of a bird. As the haiku poet Issa wrote,

> The world of dew
> is only the world of dew—
> and yet

It is this "and yet" that we carry in our hearts and where the seeming paradox comes to rest.

Precepts for Smart People

SOME FRIENDS and I were having a conversation when one of them mentioned a series of computer books with titles like *Microsoft Word for Dummies* and *Windows for Dummies*. He said that he had heard that someone was also going to write a book called *Sex for Dummies*. Another friend then quipped, "*Sex for Dummies* seems too easy. The book we need is *Sex for Smart People*." Or perhaps a more accurate title for the book we really need is *Smart Sex for Anybody*.

We can all probably recall actions we have performed that are capable of qualifying for any number of volumes written about acting unskillfully and creating suffering. The question we need to ask is: How can we avoid these kind of actions and live wisely? When we have developed clear understanding, we see that finding true happiness depends on brushing up on the "smart" volumes: *Smart Sex for All People, Smart Communication for All People, The Intelligence of Loving Yourself for All People*, or *The Wisdom of Caring for Others for All People*. Actually, the twenty-five-hundred-year-old classical Buddhist precepts can be seen as the basis of books such as these.

For laypeople there are just five basic precepts that are traditionally taught. The first is to refrain from killing any living being. Based on our caring connection for all beings, this develops a reverence in us for the totality of life. The next precept is to refrain from stealing or taking that which has not been offered. The third precept, to refrain from sexual misconduct, means refraining from using our sexual energy in a way that causes harm to ourselves or to others. The fourth is to refrain from lying and inappropriate speech, which acknowledges the power and impact of how we communicate. And the last of the five basic precepts is to refrain from taking intoxicants, such as drugs or alcohol, which cloud the mind and cause heedlessness, preventing us from experiencing the natural radiance of the mind.

The precepts essentially provide a contextual framework for spiritual life. They are not intended to be put forth as draconian laws. Abiding by the precepts allows our lives to be seamless. Being mindful of our motivations and our actions, we keep ourselves from creating unnecessary stress. Doing this, we develop a spirit of contentment, and our minds become still enough for clear seeing to arise. Without a life of mindful morality, we are missing this necessary ingredient for our inner work. Our deepest insights into happiness and lovingkindness, as well as the perception that we are all interrelated, give rise to a natural inclination that seeks to act according to the precepts.

Once during a retreat someone asked me to speak about the classical precepts. When I had finished, the person who had asked the question appeared quite upset. He said to me, "But all of that is just a way to avoid suffering! That must mean we are afraid to suffer. And that seems to run counter to Buddhism." Certainly the precepts are a way to avoid suffering—by not creating it. Doing this is not a cowardly act at all. In this world where we are all interdependent, the precepts simply acknowledge that our actions have consequences. This is not just a nice sentiment; it is a law of nature. And so in our lives, we might as well choose to be a warrior for freedom from suffering rather than be a warrior for greater suffering.

And it truly takes the courage of a warrior to move out of actions that are merely convenient or familiar or easy. *Unconscious Sex, Careless Speech, Thoughtless Action* could all be very long books, and probably many of us are qualified to write at least a few chapters for each. But regardless of our past actions, starting right now we can begin to understand more clearly and thus live in a smarter and more graceful way. With mindfulness of our behavior, rather than being driven by old habits, we can choose to pay attention to what really brings us happiness, as well as what brings happiness to others. In those areas in which we've been deluded and have suffered and caused suffering, we can choose to become more aware. In re-creating our lives in this way, we also bring stillness to our minds and to our whole way of living—so that the real treasures of the liberated mind can be revealed, shining through us.

Joyful Compassion

ONE SUMMER I attended a Buddhist-Christian conference in which the Dalai Lama was a leading participant. The event opened with a tree-planting ceremony attended by all of the religious brothers of the host monastery. I happened to be standing right next to the Dalai Lama as the ceremony was about to begin. Suddenly, across the courtyard, he spotted an extremely elderly brother in a wheelchair. Entirely disrupting the ceremony, the Dalai Lama cried out, "Oh, he's old!" and, followed by security people and television-camera operators, he raced across the courtyard to embrace the old monk. What struck me about that moment was the pleasure with which the Dalai Lama cried out, "Oh, he's old!" It was not pity; it was delight. His Holiness was celebrating the length of the old monk's life and the joy he felt at having him among us.

We often think of compassion as being brought forth by seeing suffering—and certainly that's true. But there is also a quality of compassion, a feeling of deep connection, that arises from rejoicing. Someone once asked Munindra why he practiced meditation. His students gathered around, expecting to hear an exalted, lofty answer. Munindra replied, "I practice meditation to notice the small purple flowers growing by the roadside, which I otherwise might miss." When we start to notice the small purple flowers, we come to want others to also see them, for their solace and enjoyment. Yet this is not pity but the compassionate wish to share delight.

Such joyful compassion might also arise from our delight in certain states of mind. After beginning to practice generosity or lovingkindness, we may see our minds opening up and letting go in situations where we would usually hold on, afraid of losing something precious, or wondering if we will ever get what we want. In meditation practice, we rejoice actively and even passionately in these openings and in the realizations that come to us. This rejoicing is not characterized by attachment, because we know that these experiences will, by their nature, change. It is characterized, rather, by gratitude for the capacity of a human being to open, love, care, see the truth, connect. Recognizing that all beings have this ability, joyful compassion awakens in us as the wish for others to be able to open, care, and connect, rather than remaining alone and afraid.

An important point to remember is that this compassionate wish does not come from a self-righteous perspective or from a desire to proselytize. It comes from seeing how much people want to be happy and yet how so few people truly are. The feeling of compassion grows in us when we know how the energy of love is available all around us and yet how so many people are lonely. Compassion comes from noticing the beauty of the purple flowers growing by the roadside and yet seeing how they are steadily overlooked. It comes from observing how many wise, elderly people there are among us, and how they remain unnoticed, uncelebrated. Joyful compassion comes from knowing the wonderful capacity of the human heart to connect, and wishing that more of us felt connected to each other.

Compassion born from joy comes to us and through us as an affirmation that everyone can live a meaningful, fulfilling life. "Happiness is available . . . please help yourself," says Thich Nhat Hanh. When we cross this threshold of understanding and find the wealth of happiness available to us, we realize how much we want to help all the beings in the world to come join us.

The Opportunity of Imprisonment

In 1989 Aung San Suu Kyi, leader of the pro-democracy movement in Burma, was placed under house arrest for her political activities. Suu Kyi's sons were sixteen and twelve when she was arrested, and she was not able to see them again for years. It was more than two years before she saw her husband again. While still confined, she received the Nobel Peace Prize in 1991.

Describing her imprisonment, Suu Kyi wrote, "I refused to accept anything from the military. Sometimes I didn't even have enough money to eat. I became so weak from malnourishment that my hair fell out, and I couldn't get out of bed." At the time, Aung San Suu Kyi was involved in the Buddhist practice of metta, or lovingkindness. Despite the depth of her suffering, she later said, "When I compared notes with my colleagues in the democracy movement in Burma who have suffered long terms of imprisonment, we found that an enhanced appreciation of metta was a common experience. We had known and felt both the effects of metta and the unwholesomeness of natures lacking in metta."

I think Aung San Suu Kyi's courage is extraordinary. For her to be separated from her family, facing hunger and fear, and yet view the whole ordeal in terms of enhancing her appreciation of lovingkindness—that is the embodiment of true warriorship. During her imprisonment, Suu Kyi lacked food and money, but she did have her spiritual practice.

We might feel like Suu Kyi's situation is far removed from our own circumstances, but in a way her experiences can be understood by all of us. I have talked to people imprisoned by their bodies, who were in long-term chronic pain. I have talked to people held hostage in a controlling relationship or by an unsympathetic and uncaring system that held power over them. I have talked to people in South Africa during the apartheid era who shocked me by asking about the efficacy of practicing lovingkindness while facing torture. I've known many people who were deeply and horribly afraid of someone or something in their lives. And I myself have felt completely out of control of my own life, sitting in a doctor's waiting room, seeing how life and death can turn on a dime, seeing that just existing in a body can feel like a form of imprisonment. Whatever our particular life situation, we can recognize what it feels like to be in captivity.

It is tremendously inspiring for me to see someone whose situation is frightening and full of personal loss and yet who remains steadfast in the values of her spiritual practice while accomplishing what she feels needs to be done. Seeing the courage and faith expressed in her life reminds me what our efforts for freedom are fundamentally about—to remember the goodness we are capable of and to realize it in this life. We need to realize the great strengths we have within. Suu Kyi has said, "The spiritual dimension becomes particularly important in a struggle in which deeply held convictions and strength of mind are the chief weapons against armed repression."

About a year after Aung San Suu Kyi's release from house arrest, the military dictatorship, known by the acronym of SLORC, made sweeping arrests of members of her political party. Outside her home in Rangoon, Suu Kyi told a crowd of about ten thousand that her party would not bend to pressure from the military government but would push ahead toward its goal of democracy for Burma. Rumors rapidly spread of SLORC's intention to rearrest her. Suu Kyi's comment in response was: "It will be an opportunity to strengthen my spiritual life."

The threat of reimprisonment did not make her waiver from her goal for others, or her goal for herself. Instead of deciding to give up and leave the country, return to her family and have the certainty of enough to eat, she stayed, saying: "SLORC doesn't understand how helpful my years of house arrest were to me. If I'm arrested, we will go forward; if I'm not arrested, we will go forward." Aung San Suu Kyi remains essentially free, even if in prison. She knows this, and we must know it too, regarding the imprisoning conditions of our own lives: it is this vision of freedom that we need, so that we do not lose sight of our spiritual goals while facing our own situation, doing whatever it is that we need to do.

The Heart of Forgiveness

AT A COURSE I was teaching in Israel, I led a guided meditation on forgiveness. Afterward, one of the participants approached me to say that he had felt overwhelmed by the forgiveness practice. Throughout the course I noticed him adjusting his position often during the meditation periods, and I had wondered if he had some kind of painful physical condition that made it hard for him to sit still. In speaking with me, he revealed that he had survived a recent terrorist attack in which someone had opened fire randomly with a shotgun on a street corner. He was in frequent pain because not all of the fragments of buckshot could be removed from his body. With profound emotion, the man said, "I don't know if it is possible to learn to forgive. However, I do know that it is possible, and in fact essential, to learn to stop hating."

On hearing that, I wondered if stopping hating and learning to forgive were not really the same thing. Often, we confuse forgiveness with forgetting or condoning or denying a terrible reality. Yet to forgive is not any of these things. As part of the practice of the forgiveness meditation, we say, "Just as I wish to be forgiven, I forgive those who have hurt or harmed me." When we say these words, we take a radically different stance in regard to someone who has harmed us. We may be saying, "I let go of seeing you solely as the perpetrator of such and such an action." But this does not mean that we are condoning that action or saying, "It's all right that you did that." We still remember clearly what happened, and the pain of it. Or we may let go of identifying ourselves solely as "a person who was hurt" and realize that we are much bigger than that. Or we may recognize, like that meditator during the retreat in Israel, that taking a position of hatred only destroys us, and if we are to live our lives fully, we must learn to let go of hatred. To stop hating makes room for love to arise.

Many of us have seen the famous Vietnam War photograph of a little child running, her body aflame from napalm. When her village temple was bombed by South Vietnamese, she was engulfed in the flames. The little girl, Kim Phuc, who was nine years old at the time, survived. Kim Phuc says she can forgive but will never forget what happened. She still has terrible nightmares and, of course, visible scars. "Even when I see the picture I can't imagine why they did it to children, to innocent people. The children didn't do anything. Why did they have to suffer?" Her eyes brimming with tears, she goes on, "The war happened, but in the past. I want to say to the pilot, 'We have to love each other.' I can forgive."

Horrifying, cruel things happen in the world. It is the height of delusion to deny that these things occur. The question is: How do we respond when we are the recipients of cruelty? Forgiveness obviously does not have to do with denying our suffering or our anger but with opening to something greater. When we do so, we discover the self-destructiveness of our hatred and, simultaneously, our extraordinary capacity for love. Whether or not we ever call it forgiveness, to recognize that place of clear seeing, of openheartedness, is a heroic journey.

Maha Ghosananda, who is the Supreme Patriarch of Cambodian Buddhism, was in Thailand when the Khmer Rouge began the terrible bloodshed in Cambodia. He was acting as a translator at a temple where a friend of mine happened to be practicing. On first hearing news of the killing, Maha Ghosananda grabbed my friend's arm and

choked out the words, "The streets are going to be running
with blood." Appallingly, he was right. Maha Ghosananda
is one of the few Cambodian monks who survived those
times.

In 1978, Maha Ghosananda greeted the first influx of
Cambodian refugees to the camps on the Thai border. He
reminded them of the Buddha's words, "Hatred will never
cease by hatred. Hatred can only cease by love." For the
next two years, he worked to establish Buddhist temples in
each refugee camp on the Thai-Cambodian border.

At a conference in the United States in 1996, he was
asked numerous times to describe the work he had done in
the camps, what his goals were, and the methodology he
used to achieve them. In answer to each question, Maha
Ghosananda would quietly reply, "I was making peace with
myself. . . . I was making peace with myself. . . . When you
make peace with yourself, you make peace with the world."

Perhaps the essence of forgiveness is just that—making
peace with ourselves. We make peace with our outrage, with
our helplessness, with our anger and resentment. For it
seems that forgiveness has more to do with ourselves than
with others. Once we have made peace with all of those
painful aspects of ourselves, we can cease hating, and we
can allow love to come forth. "When you make peace with
yourself, you make peace with the world."

The Blessing of Presence

WHEN THE DALAI LAMA was leaving the Tucson hotel where a conference had been held, it seemed as if the entire staff, hundreds of people, lined up to say good-bye to him. The lobby was filled with maids and chefs and gardeners and security personnel; people of many different races, ethnic backgrounds, ages, and most likely, various religious affiliations. Most of those there would probably never call themselves Buddhists or relate to the Dalai Lama as a personal teacher, but each was seeming to find a kind of blessing in merely being with him.

The Dalai Lama walked down the line, greeting each person, smiling, looking in their eyes, thanking them for their service. Many people wept; many looked at him completely enraptured. At no time did I get the impression that his attention was wandering or that he would rather have been somewhere else. Without exception, he was fully attentive to each person as he met them. The effect of this wholehearted presence was remarkable.

Being in the proximity of the Dalai Lama, and others of the community of beings committed to the truth, is an experience of feeling greatly blessed. A major component of the blessing power of such beings is that sometimes, without a single word exchanged, they remind us of what we are all capable of. Often we forget or cannot imagine the depth and richness of our own inner life, of our inner strength. Mirrored by these beings, we renew our belief in ourselves, moving beyond our conditioned and limited views of our own abilities.

Their very being says to us again and again, "Freedom is possible. Love is possible. Deep compassion is possible." It feels as if there is a fire within them, ablaze with possibilities, that can, in turn, light a fire within us. The urgent desire within them to be truthful, to wake up, not to waste their lives, brings forth a quality of urgency within us as well. Their ability to love moves us to be vehicles of love ourselves. The depth of peace within them and their unshakable confidence in the teachings awakens a similar peace and confidence within us.

I find that being in the presence of such people evokes a sense of timelessness. Sometimes it feels to me like I am joining a great stream. I feel the women and the men and the children who for so many years, so many centuries, have walked a spiritual path, have gone forth into the unknown, have let go of habitual tendencies, have challenged conventional ways of thinking, have gone beyond the familiar, and have seen the truth. Inspired by them, we join in the courage of all those who have taken risks and made a commitment to the truth. Human beings just like us, they are the loving reminders of the possibility of realizing our own aspirations to be free.

Looking around at those gathered in the hotel lobby that day in Tucson, I recalled a visit to the former Soviet Union I had made in the eighties. At the time, religious observance was not common, so when married couples left the registry office, they would go to lay wreaths of flowers on a national monument, such as Lenin's tomb. Sometimes I would be in front of the tomb for much of the day, and every hour I saw dozens of couples, the bride dressed in full bridal gown and veil, the groom in formal attire, arrive one after another to perform this ceremony. Watching them, I reflected that perhaps there is something inviolate within us that seeks the sacred, that looks for a way to consecrate our lives, whatever the circumstances may be.

Being with a completely present, deeply compassionate person is itself an experience of consecration. It honors our own highest potential to fully enter into the moment, to love without exception, and to be free. In the lobby of that hotel in Tucson, the presence of the Dalai Lama sparked an awareness that I could be a more compassionate and loving person. We can all mirror for others their lovability and their capacity for freedom. This is our intimate connection with the stream of courageous beings who have found a deeper truth in their lives.

Truth-Telling

SOMETIMES on the spiritual journey we adopt a self-conscious persona, trying to be someone we are not or to feel things that we don't actually feel. If we like the idea of ourselves as being loving and compassionate, it might be very difficult for us to acknowledge all of those moments when we are not really loving or compassionate. Our aspiration to be "someone spiritual" can often get in the way of our telling the truth to ourselves about what we're feeling. Thinking that we are only supposed to have loving and compassionate feelings can be a terrible obstacle to spiritual practice. In this vein, I used to say that since the title of my first book was *Lovingkindness*, the title of my next book, the companion "shadow" volume, should be *The Tyranny of Lovingkindness*.

Kamala Masters, a Buddhist meditation teacher, was once sailing with some friends off one of the islands of Hawaii. She began to feel quite seasick, and her friends urged her to get into the ocean to relieve the queasiness. Not having a life vest, Kamala was reluctant to do so, but her friends persuaded her and a few of them jumped overboard with her. A few minutes after they got into the water a sudden squall blew up. Those on the sailboat couldn't lower the sails fast enough, nor could they get the engine started. Kamala watched helplessly as the boat blew away!

She began to panic, fearing that she would drown. Her friends surrounded her, and knowing how important the Buddha's teachings are to her, they asked her: "Kamala, what if these are your last moments? What do you want right now? Don't you want more love in your heart? Don't you want more compassion? What do you really want?" Kamala has dedicated her life to the Buddha's teaching, and in this dire moment, she had an excellent opportunity to display the depth of her devotion. In her persona as a teacher, she might have answered that it was, of course, love and compassion that she wanted right then in her last moments of life. But, fundamentally dedicated to the truth, Kamala thought for a second and, from the bottom of her heart, said, "What I want right now is the boat!"

Sometimes, no matter what the degree of our aspiration, all we really want is just to have the boat back. But we might be reluctant to express the truth of this, if we feel the need to project a certain image of ourselves. "Kamala is a meditation teacher, so there must be only lofty thoughts in her mind." Attached to a persona, we may be driven by ideas of what others expect of us, whether they are current acquaintances or figures of mythic proportion, such as the Buddha. To be driven by the actual expectations of others, let alone by what we imagine they might expect, is like trying to squeeze ourselves into a suit made for someone else, only to see that we are not able to breathe or move freely at all.

If we take on this "tyranny of aspiration," we will likely

set up a dynamic of resistance and resentment toward our states of inner suffering. "I don't want it to be this way. I can't accept this. It shouldn't be this way. I'm on the spiritual path, and I should have let go of this long ago. Spiritual people never feel this kind of thing." All of our energy is used up in this struggle, and there is no possibility of moving beyond it. However, when we relate with openness and presence to our suffering, whatever the cause may be, we find that we actually do have the energy to move beyond it.

Being truthful about what is actually happening in our minds does not mean that we should not aspire to act with love and awareness. Our whole lives can rightfully be dedicated to that effort. But the Buddha's teaching on Right Effort is founded on the open acknowledgment of what is actually happening in any moment. If this understanding is not there, we act from a basis of avoidance, and this only leads us into further suffering. Then we will find it difficult to sincerely move into a place of love and compassion. Inside of us, there will be that inconvenient and unacceptable shadow lingering, no matter how we try to overlook it.

The End of the Path

INDIA abounds in teachers and gurus and spiritual paths of every description. For some, this caused confusion and conflict; for others, it was intriguing. When I was studying with Munindra in Bodh-gaya, my fellow students would occasionally approach him and say that they were interested in going off and exploring another religious tradition, or that they wanted to meet some other teacher. I was struck by Munindra's openness. He would consistently encourage them to go. When asked by surprised onlookers why he did so, Munindra quietly stated, "The Dharma doesn't suffer from comparison."

Truth is truth. There is no way that it can be divided into little pieces and claimed as an emblem of belonging, or of private, personal excellence. We suffer from comparison, not the Dharma. We suffer from being proprietary about the truth, from feeling exclusive and competitive. The teachings are not something to hold on to, defend, or prove superior. We don't need to become attached to them, as if they were a commodity we could retain as "ours." Ultimately, there is only our own life and the choice that the teachings offer to live it wisely or to remain in ignorance. This is the essence of the Buddha's practice: our heart's release from suffering, not the adoption of a sectarian identification

The body of teachings and practice and the living example of the Buddha were classically known as *Buddhadharma*, the way of the Buddha. The label of "Buddhism," as a doctrine or system of beliefs, is a relatively recent Western innovation and is not really accurate. Following the Buddhadharma does not mean adopting an "ism," adhering to a dogma, or assuming a self-identity that serves to make one feel separate or apart. It is not a question of belief. Nor is it simply a way to follow in the footsteps of the historical Buddha. It is a means for us to recognize our innate wisdom and limitless compassion.

When there is attachment to a belief system, there is the need to defend it. The Buddha himself refused to engage in the debates about religious dogma that were popular in his time. He said at one point, "It is not I who argues with the world, but the world that argues with me." In the richness of his realization and compassion, he actually exhorted his followers to let go of all entangling identifications, including the burden of identifying with one's own path. He described his own teachings as a raft we use to traverse the river of suffering until we arrive at the other shore of peace. Once we have arrived there, we just let go of the raft. We do not continue to carry it around with us.

Rigid identification with a system of beliefs arises in part from uncertainty and fear. When we don't feel connected to a personal sense of the truth, we become uneasy and cling to narrow views. If we feel deluded or confused we become frightened and look for something to hold on to, some kind of security somewhere. This is the picture of dogmatism, fanaticism, and conceit.

The spiritual righteousness born of sectarian views provokes an immense feeling of separateness, of "us" and "them," of "being better than," which in the end proves to be a self-constructed prison, a highly decorated cage. By clinging to spiritual views in such a way, we use the mystery and beauty of spirituality as an object of exploitation, rather than as the key to immeasurable love.

To let go of clinging to views, we first have to openly acknowledge the fear giving rise to this tendency. When we face our own fear, we can trace it back to our inner confusion. When, through practice, we perceive the truth of existence, and we see impermanence, suffering, and emptiness of self, we no longer feel it necessary to defend or tenaciously cling to dogma. We can freely rest in the truth. Our hearts are moved by our suffering and the suffering of others; we do not want to cultivate a feeling of separation from anyone. As Munindra said, "The Dharma doesn't suffer from comparison." And we don't have to suffer from comparison, because we don't have to stake a proprietary claim on the truth. The truth will sustain us, we don't have to sustain it.

The Buddhadharma offers a way to live that proves its own validity, just in the practice of it. Thus, it is not a belief to be defended but a guide for transformation. On our personal journey of discovery, we see that attachment to the way that we walk is not at all the point; it is the truth itself that is the purpose of following the path. The end of deluded attachment to all things, including the path, is the end of the path.

Responsibility

I WAS BORN JEWISH in the 1950s. My childhood was permeated with the effects of the Holocaust. Family members often spoke of survivors, starvation, death and madness, relatives killed in front of their children. Of course, this talk was always in the context of "those people over there who did it." It wasn't until I visited the Holocaust Museum in Washington, D.C., that I came to a different, and unexpected, understanding.

I found the museum shocking, and it was painful to contemplate the horrors of those years as I viewed the various exhibits. I had expected that response in myself. What I did not expect was how reluctant I was to look at the exhibits implicating U.S. and British immigration policies as collusive with the Nazi regime. After all, Jews who had been allowed to emigrate would not have been slaughtered. I did not really want to believe that the Holocaust had anything to do with my own country. Whatever the United States might have done further back in history or does right now, it was far easier for me to think that in terms of the Holo-caust, "they did it." I wanted to believe that the moral re-sponsibility for extermination of targeted populations had nothing to do with my country, nothing to do with me, nothing to do with anyone I know.

But it does. That day at the Holocaust Museum I had to acknowledge that I live in a country that contributed to the Holocaust. I realized the folly of declaring anyone to be the "other." The things we do, or fail to do, don't just disap-pear, but reverberate out through the vast web of our inter-connectedness. We are all intricately involved with one another, whether we realize it or not. This understanding is not about taking on a burden of guilt; it is about the realiza-tion that whatever each one of us does matters. The actions we take in our daily lives can make a difference, not only for ourselves but for others as well.

Inscribed on a wall of the museum was a striking quota-tion, attributed to a German pastor named Martin Niemöl-ler. It says: "First they came for the Socialists, and I did not speak out because I was not a Socialist. Then they came for the trade unionists, and I did not speak out because I was not a trade unionist. Then they came for the Jews, and I did not speak out because I was not a Jew. Then they came for me, and there was no one left to speak for me."

What was so tremendously moving and, ironically, em-powering about this experience was that when I saw the Holocaust simply in terms of "them" doing it, I felt like there was nothing I could do to keep "them" from doing it again. But when I realized that my choices do make a difference—because we are interdependent, and what each of us does affects everyone else in some way—I realized the power of taking responsibility. Wisdom arising from clear seeing recognizes that we are all connected to one another, that no one stands alone, that what we do makes a difference. Compassion transforms that vision into motivation to act for the sake of others. If we take care of others, others will take care of us, and "otherness" itself will drop away.

Ready to Die

AUNG SAN SUU KYI was walking down a village road with a few of her followers when some soldiers jumped out of a jeep, crouched down, aimed their guns at her, and prepared to fire on the orders of their captain. Suu Kyi waved away her supporters and walked toward the soldiers alone. She later said, "It seemed so much simpler to provide them with a single target than to bring everyone else in." At the last minute a superior officer arrived on the scene and rescinded the orders.

Suu Kyi later said, "I've never thought of myself as particularly fearless." Courage, she commented further, "comes from cultivating the habit of refusing to let fear dictate one's actions." By facing her fear head-on, Suu Kyi was able, despite any fear she might have felt, to do that which she deeply believed had to be done.

Aung San Suu Kyi, armed with the determination to end political oppression in her country, has surrendered her own freedom and safety. Throughout the years of her detention, the military offered to release her, but only if she would leave Burma and live in exile. She has always refused. Many of her own supporters have urged her to leave and to continue her work for the cause of democracy outside the country, where she would be safer. But she has not left. Upon being released after six years of house arrest, Suu Kyi said in an interview, "Well, I knew I was not going to give up, but there was always the possibility that I would die before they released me."

I once helped lead a meditation retreat for social activists, and among them were a few people who had been homeless before getting involved in social work. One participant was a former junkie who had survived for years as a mugger. We asked him how he approached people he intended to rob. What was in his mind? Did he have a technique? He replied, "No, no technique, but as I went up to people, I found that place inside me that was completely ready to die, and I, without a word, let that be known. That's what cowed people. My greatest weapon was the fact that I was not afraid to die."

Two people, Aung San Suu Kyi and the mugger, both committed to their objectives, however different they may be, and both ready to die. The former mugger says he was not afraid to die, and it gave him the capacity to put himself in precarious positions and to hurt others. Aung San Suu Kyi says that while she might have been fearful in confronting her adversaries, she did so anyway, even though it might mean her death, and it gave her the capacity to serve others. Both have apparently gone beyond fear, but there is a fundamental difference in the nature of their fearlessness.

We can imagine we are fearless, ready to die because we are trapped in a bleak and desolate world, cut off from our feelings and limited to personal survival. Or we can be actually fearless and ready to die because we have discovered the deepest sense of what it means to be alive. We can be truly fearless only when, with a spacious and compassionate heart, we are profoundly in touch with our innermost fear; when we are mindful of it, are not hating ourselves for the fear, and are not being ruled by it. This is the distinctive power of mindfulness. Our choices are not dictated by feelings that we are not conscious of—feelings that obscure our vision of truth.

Committed to easing suffering in the world, Aung San Suu Kyi's course of action was made clear. Strengthened by mindfulness, she is able to say "The only real prison is fear, and the only real freedom is freedom from fear."

Step by Step

In the early eighties, Joseph Goldstein and I went to Zimbabwe to teach. Our students there sent us on a trip to Victoria Falls and the area around it. One evening at dusk, Joseph and I set out in a small boat with a guide, floating down the Zambezi River, watching the sunset, hearing the extraordinary sounds of the native animals on the shores. It was a scene of tremendous beauty. I felt as if I had come upon the beginning of time, to find myself in the midst of the wondrousness of creation. The rest of the world and all its troubles simply disappeared.

After some time Joseph asked our guide if we could pull over to the shore and take a walk while there was still light. The guide's response abruptly ended my idyllic fantasies. He said, "That whole shore is laced with land mines from the civil war. Animals regularly get blown apart. Many children who have wandered there are dead or are missing limbs. Better not." Better not indeed. Drifting down the Zambezi River, my perceptions began to shift to include the horror of the hidden dangers there, in the midst of "paradise."

I have since learned that more than a hundred million

land mines are scattered across some sixty countries of the world. Long after armies have vacated the battlefields and the political tides have turned, the still-hidden mines continue to devastate people's lives on a massive scale. Land mines do not discriminate between an approaching enemy soldier and a playful child, between a dangerous intruder and a naive tourist taking a walk. More than a thousand people are killed by mines every month, and many more are injured or permanently disabled. Financially, clearing a minefield costs at least a hundred times what it took to lay it in the ground, and it is obviously a very dangerous operation. Consequently, the mines largely remain uncleared.

There is an international grassroots petition being circulated for signatures, requesting that all countries stop the production and use of land mines. Every year Maha Ghosananda, a Cambodian monk and nominee for the Nobel Peace Prize, leads peace marches through Cambodia to collect signatures for the ban. After decades of bloodshed and civil war, Cambodia is one of the world's most heavily mined countries. Land mines make almost half the land area of Cambodia unsafe for farming or any other human use, and the country has the world's highest percentage of people disabled through land mine explosions. Cambodia has also contributed more signatures to the petition than any other nation. Often a signature is a thumbprint in red ink, because so many of the people are illiterate.

At each stop along the peace march, Maha Ghosananda gives a simple Dharma talk about "the necessity of removing the land mines in our hearts: greed, hatred, delusion, as they are the source of the land mines in the ground." These forces may lie hidden within us, perhaps behind a manicured facade of ease. But when someone does something to us that we do not like, or certain circumstances arise, then they explode, tragically harming others and ourselves.

Just as it is much easier to lay the land mines in the ground than it is to get them out, so is it also true of habits cultivated unconsciously. Just as the land mines in the ground were the result of unconscious actions, done without thinking of the long-term consequences, so do we, in our daily lives, engage in acts of greed, hatred, or delusion, unconscious of the long-term consequences.

It takes tremendous courage to step away from these familiar, habitual patterns of acting, but it can be done. I often feel empowered when I remember the Buddha's words: "If it were not possible, I would not ask you to do it."

Given the prevalence of land mines in Cambodia, and the political forces at work there, there is some danger involved for the marchers who set out on peace walks, like the ones that Maha Ghosananda leads. In 1994 the march was caught in cross fire between government and Democratic Kampuchea soldiers. One monk and one nun were killed, and three walkers were wounded. At a conference in 1996, when Maha Ghosananda was asked how he helped people who walked with him overcome their fear of explosions or being caught in cross fire, he said, "I tell them we will simply go together, step-by-step."

In our own journey to remove the habitual tendencies of greed, hatred, and delusion, we often find power in solidarity. We can help each other do together what any one of us might feel that we cannot do alone. In Buddhist texts, "having good friends" is emphasized as a strong contributing force to sustaining positive qualities, such as love or wisdom. Having good friends, teachers, mentors, and community helps us by providing a sense of solidarity, shared values, supporting one another, of inspiring and reminding one another.

Maha Ghosananda has said, "Our journey for peace begins today and every day. We shall never be discouraged. We shall walk slowly, slowly, step-by-step. Each step will be a prayer." We can only make this journey to remove the land mines, the inner ones or the outer ones, step-by-step. Each step weaves a small part of the tapestry of the journey. Going together, we can do a lot to ease our own suffering and to help ease the suffering in this world.

Seeing Deeply

AUNG SAN SUU KYI has pointed out that "those who have had to face persistent political persecution become highly politicized. Our lives take on a rhythm different from those who, on waking up in the morning, do not need to wonder who might have been arrested during the night and what further acts of blatant injustice might be committed against our people later during the day. Our antennae become highly sensitive to vibrations barely noticed by those whose everyday existence is removed from political strife." This level of sensitivity, developed in response to danger, is one known by many whose lives are bound in suffering daily. Just as that sensitivity serves to impel us to reach for safety, it can also become a tool on the path to spiritual liberation.

Those who were abused as children, and those who are adult children of alcoholics, often describe in a similar way becoming highly sensitive to what is going on around them. This extreme sensitivity arises from the fact that they, too, like those who face constant political persecution, did not know what injustices might be carried out against them, or when. Children who are raised in an atmosphere of trauma learn to see the subtle signs of danger, to look for unspoken yet real threats. They feel the hidden realities existing in their homes—realities that might go unseen by friends and neighbors.

Adults who are disempowered in our society—disenfranchised minorities and stigmatized groups—often describe this same heightened sensitivity. They become accustomed to reading the nonverbal channels of communication that may hint of danger: tones of voice, gestures, and facial expressions that are incongruent with the words spoken. In situations in which they have little power to actively guide the course of events, they are forced to remain highly attuned, just to protect themselves.

Of course, everyone's life contains something of the circumstances that create this faculty of sensitivity. All relationships are a shifting tide of balances and imbalances. Much of reality is hidden, unspoken, inexpressible. Life is full of passages into the unknown, places that are mysterious and frightening. We often enter them with our antennae finely tuned to the possibility of danger.

Sensitivity to the unknown can be used not just defensively to anticipate potential dangers, but also spiritually to discern levels of reality not apparent at a casual glance. When we explore the circumstances around us with our awareness attuned to sensing what is really true, we more finely direct our efforts to overcoming ignorance; consequently, we are able to awaken to the full richness of our lives. For those whose lives have necessitated developing such sensitivity—even though it may have come because of great suffering—this can lead to profound personal healing.

No matter what we may have experienced during our lives, we can find a refuge in spiritual truth, where nothing has to be kept hidden or remain secret. Having found a genuine refuge, we can take the talents that might have been born in fear and courageously use them to open continuously to a deeper reality. Having discovered safety within, we also discover the faith to risk this opening.

Those who have been badly hurt or marginalized in some way may actually act as powerful teachers for us, reminding us to try to look more deeply into everything. They can lead the way to naming injustice as injustice, to recovering the forgotten, to remembering what or who is being overlooked. They can challenge us to see that no one and no thing should rightfully be left out of our awareness.

Very Happy

ONE OF MY TEACHERS, Nyoshul Khen Rinpoche (called Khenpo by his students), was one of the many thousands of Tibetans who fled their country in 1959 because of the Chinese invasion of Tibet and the terrible religious persecution that followed. In Tibet, Khenpo had been a high lama and an heir to all of the sacred teachings of the different schools and lineages of Tibetan Buddhism. During a retreat he taught in the United States many years after he left Tibet, he began telling us the story of how he had left his family behind, not knowing if he would ever see them again, as he set out for India with about seventy other people.

One night, as the group traveled through the mountains, Chinese soldiers ambushed them, showering them with machine gun bullets. Only five people survived the attack and escaped on foot through treacherous Himalayan passes to India. Soon after arriving, Khenpo went to Calcutta and found a place to sleep in a Buddhist monastery. He spoke to us about begging for pennies on the streets of Calcutta, just so he could have a cup of tea to drink.

It was heart wrenching to hear Khenpo speak about those traumatic circumstances: the Chinese persecution—the humiliation, torture, and death of so many Tibetans; the sorrow of leaving loved ones behind; the slaughter of Khenpo's companions; the sheer physical brutality of the escape. The image of this teacher, whom I love so much, begging for pennies, deprived of all physical comforts, was overwhelming for me to hear. As I began to cry, I noticed that several other people in the room were also crying.

Just at that point, Khenpo finished up his story of begging in Calcutta with the phrase, "And I was very happy." My mind came to an abrupt stop. Very happy? Did he say, "very happy"? I could scarcely believe he had said that! The man was bereft, poverty-stricken, a refugee—how could he say he was "very happy"?

As Khenpo went on, he talked about being sustained through all these events and sudden turns of fate by the truth of the Buddha's teaching. He had gone from being an esteemed religious teacher in Tibet, with great distinction and honor, addressing multitudes of spiritual aspirants, to finding himself suddenly begging in the hot streets of Calcutta, surrounded by poverty and hopelessness. Then, later on, he went from the crowds of India to the United States, where he was again received as a highly revered teacher. "So many unexpected ups and downs—who can describe them?" Khenpo said. "Isn't life like a series of dreams within a vast, dreamlike mirage?" After his talk, my mind was still reeling. Every so often, if we are fortunate, we catch a glimpse of a quality of happiness or freedom in another human being that is not bound to conditions, that sustains them even through extraordinary suffering. Khenpo's intense love and devotion for the Buddha's teachings had borne the fruit of this deep happiness, right in the midst of his inconceivable challenges.

Khenpo's inner peace in the midst of these difficult circumstances did not diminish the reality of what had happened to him—the suffering that he and others had experienced when he fled into exile—nor did Khenpo's reaction contain even a trace of complacency about the pain of the other refugees, beggars, or the poverty-stricken people he encountered in Calcutta. Even though Khenpo was "very happy" and peaceful in the midst of his suffering, he was not oblivious to the anguish of others; he remained intensely dedicated to helping fellow Tibetans and to bringing the teachings of the Buddha to others. Khenpo's happiness is a celebration of the Buddha's teachings, a celebration of the human spirit, and a reminder of the possibility of our own unlimited joy.

The Presence of Patience

DURING the first few weeks after opening the Insight Meditation Society, we received numerous requests for information. Among these letters were two that were especially memorable for how they were addressed. One had been written to "The Hindsight Meditation Society," seeming to suggest either that our vision was perfectly 20/20 or that we started IMS as an afterthought. The other, which I found even more intriguing, was addressed to "The Instant Meditation Society." How wonderful! I imagined a package of dehydrated meditation to which one would just add a bit of water and then mix together for instant peace of mind. What's funny about this, of course, is that the only "instant" part of meditation is *this* instant—and then the next instant, and then the next. And the most important ingredient in "instant meditation," in this sense, is patience.

True patience is constancy—the consistent willingness to use this moment of reality as a vehicle for wisdom and compassion. Patience is not about gritting one's teeth and saying, "I'll bear with this for another five minutes because I'm sure it will be over by then and something better will come along." Patience is not dour, and it is not unhappy. It is a genuine connection with whatever is happening right now. Patience is a great power. The Buddha talked about it as being both the highest austerity and the highest form of devotion.

Patience is a steadfast strength that we apply to each moment. It does not imply a sense of succumbing to, a complacent giving up, or even an endless standing by. Patience does not mean being enslaved by the moment; nor does it mean that we must accept whatever comes without ever taking action to change things. If the moment requires taking some kind of relevant action, we must do so. What is most important is the way in which we take action. Patience is actually quite simple. It means a full and open connection to the moment—a connection that involves tremendous integrity.

Our cultural consciousness is so focused on things happening instantly that it is a significant endeavor for us to cultivate this sort of wholeheartedness in each moment. We always seem to be looking ahead to what will happen next.

A friend once told me a story about a vegetable garden he had when he was a young child. In the garden he planted carrots, but he would get so excited when he saw the little green shoots that he would pull the carrots up out of the ground to see how they were doing. The practice of patience is learning to be present in the moment while things take their own time.

This is the kind of patience we bring to meditation practice. My teacher Munindra used to say: "In meditation practice, time is not a factor. It is not something that is relevant in this process. Practice is timeless." To place spiritual practice in a context of time means anticipation, disappointment, expectation, and betrayal. It is like planting a garden and trying to make carrots grow faster than they actually can grow. They grow in their own time and in their own way. We plant the seed, we nurture it, we water it, we let it be.

In our daily lives, the heart of patience might manifest as the resolution to simply do what needs to be done. I have a friend whose young daughter was diagnosed with a brain tumor. The tumor was benign but was situated in such a way as to be considered deadly. Two surgeries, one of them eleven hours long, did not manage to remove the tumor. My friend took her daughter to a well-known neurologist, who told her it was hopeless. He estimated that—after a steady, unremitting physical and mental decline—my friend's beautiful daughter would die within two years.

My friend didn't give up but patiently and determinedly continued to look for treatments. She found a neurologist who suggested a particular type of radiation. That treatment, in combination with some other methods, began shrinking the tumor. When the tests first showed that the tumor was decreasing in size, the doctor along with everyone else in the room burst into tears. Eventually, there was no trace of a tumor at all. When I praised my friend for not giving up, for optimistically looking for new treatments for her daughter, she said she only did what she had to do, one moment at a time. This is patience.

No matter what our circumstances may be, the ability to be with each moment, to do what we have to do, and to let the process unfold, is truly one of our greatest strengths. Whether in our lives or in our meditation practice, we are supported by the courageous dedication to patience and the willingness to be present in this moment of our lives.

The Happiness of Giving

A FRIEND of mine had a grandfather who emigrated to America around the turn of the century. This man, like many others from Eastern Europe, arrived in New York by boat and ended up on Ellis Island. He had made the journey with a dear friend of his, whose destination was a different part of the United States. They loved each other very much, and before parting company they wanted to give each other something as a remembrance. However, both had absolutely nothing but the clothing they wore; neither of them had any possessions to give to the other—until they found one thing. Each unclipped his own name-tag, with his new American name written on it, and gave this to the other. By exchanging their names, their actual identities, they were in a way sharing their unknown futures; they would remain connected through all of the possibilities that were to unfold through the coming generations.

I love this story because it so wonderfully expresses the

fact that we always have something we can offer, and that the greatest gift is our willingness to connect with someone else's life—to care about them. Generosity is born of our spirit and has little to do with whether or not we have material goods to give. In India and Burma I was the recipient of incredible generosity from many people who had very little materially to offer. Some cultures, on the other hand, are rich in material goods and more reticent in giving. A recent study has shown that Los Angeles, with one of the highest percentages of wealthy citizens, falls very near the bottom in measures of philanthropy. Minneapolis, which is a fairly middle-class city, is at the top of the list. The generosity that we are all capable of is a matter of the heart.

The Buddha said that no true spiritual life is possible without this kind of generous heart. Generosity, the Buddha taught, is the primary quality of an awakened mind. The practice of generosity frees us from the sense of isolation that arises from clinging and attachment. When we believe we are alone, our hearts constrict. Then it is difficult to feel good about ourselves and we think that we have nothing special to offer. Further, because we are looking outside ourselves for something or someone to give us a sense of completion, we miss the degree to which we are already whole and complete.

When the intention to give arises in us, there is often a feeling of fear that is revealed as well. There might be fear of our own lack of abundance or of our gift's being dismissed. We may think, "I have nothing that is worth anything to give anybody," or, "Once I win the lottery I can be generous, but I can't possibly give anything at all right now." With mindfulness, however, we can see that our fears are transparent, they have no unyielding solidity, and they do not need to hold us back. When we see that these fears are conditioned thoughts that need not determine our actions, we start to see the extraordinary capacity of generosity that is in us.

True giving is a thoroughly joyous thing to do. We experience happiness when we form the intention to give, in the actual act of giving, and in the recollection of the fact that we have given. Generosity is a celebration. When we give something to someone, we feel connected to them, and our commitment to the path of peace and awareness deepens. The movement of the heart as we practice generosity in the outer world mirrors the movement of the heart when we let go of conditioned views about ourselves on our inner journey. Letting go creates a joyful sense of space in our minds. In this way our inner work and our outer work join together to create a generosity of the spirit that is the expression of freedom.

Wonderment

WHEN I first went to India in 1970, I went overland through Europe, Turkey, Iran, Afghanistan, and Pakistan before arriving in India. I was eighteen years old, and I had never traveled more than a few hundred miles from my home in New York City. I remember when I arrived at the banks of the Bosporus Strait in Turkey, which divides Europe and Asia. I stood looking over the water toward Asia, wondering what it would be like and feeling a tremendous sense of awe and adventure. Standing on the bank of that river, I had no idea that the people and cultures and spiritual traditions of Asia would become the center of my life. I only knew that I was looking for a greater happiness, and I was willing to open to whatever might come.

This sense of openness and wonder is very much like the approach we need to take in the practice of meditation. Our wonderment gives us the courage to journey, to let go of what we know and go into the unfamiliar. The world of silence and intuitive understanding that we enter in meditation is perhaps unlike any place we have known before. It is not filled with static bits of knowledge that we become attached to or use to protect ourselves from fully experiencing our lives.

And like many journeys, meditation is not a linear, step-by-step process; we don't always know exactly where we are going or even what we are going after. There is a teaching story I heard in Burma about a hunter who goes into the forest to try to capture a bird. He wanders for a long time in the forest, and in the end, he never captures the bird. But that is all right, because in the course of all that wandering, he has learned the ways of the forest. It is just like that for us in meditation. We may have the idea that there is something we would like to capture, perhaps something we can show off. But any meditation experience we can reify doesn't matter. What matters is that we are open to learning the ways of the body and the mind. What matters is that we learn how to explore, how to make this journey of discovery in harmony with our connection to all beings.

As we learn to see through the conventions of our ordinary ways of looking at things, we may for a while be more aware of what we have lost than what we've found. Once I was traveling back to the East Coast from New Mexico with some friends and their four-year-old child. In the St. Louis airport, the child unaccountably wandered off and got lost. We were all frantically running around looking for her. Finally, over the loudspeaker came the announcement: "Would you please come find your daughter at Gate 2." When we got there, we found the child very upset and frightened. She said to her mother, "You weren't where you were supposed to be." In fact, her mother had never left where she was supposed to be, and the child herself had wandered off. The incident reminded me of the betrayal and fear we sometimes feel in our lives when we discover that happiness isn't where we had expected it to be. We have been told that happiness will definitely be found in certain things: in a relationship, in a job, in money, in a particular place. And so, when we are not happy, we think that we must be lost. We think there must be something wrong with us rather than some problem with the road we've taken. Through meditation, however, we can see that there are other places that we might not have been told about, where joy and contentment also reside. And so we are free to leave behind our old patterns and entrapments, in order to walk into a new landscape.

When we approach life with wonderment, it gives us the courage to open our hearts further and further, so we can find a greater happiness than we have ever known before. There is magic in wonderment, in making a friend of silence, in the space between breaths, in finding the beautiful gift of connectedness. Through meditation practice we come to know these hidden things, to reclaim forgotten gifts.

We don't always have words for what happens to us in meditation. That is just as well, since sometimes words just serve to codify what is changing and alive. The dancer Isadora Duncan once said: "If I could tell you what it meant, there would be no point in dancing it." We can't capture freedom as a personal trophy, we can only be free; we can't reify it, we can only dance it. When we worry about what certain experiences mean, when we try to figure them out and explain them, we end up creating a sense of distance and using our knowledge as a way of preventing openness.

Bringing a sense of wonderment to our lives through meditation enables us to dance with whatever we experience, as we move into the unknown and the unfamiliar. In the Taoist tradition there is a saying:

> Approach it and there is no beginning;
> follow it and there is no end.
> You can't know it, but you can be it,
> at ease in your own life.

Going Forward

I CRIED when Dipa Ma died, thinking, "No one will ever love me like that again." What I have found instead is that the legacy of love she left behind has remained a part of me. The inspiration of her words and actions still guides my life, motivating my practice, teaching me as I teach others.

One of my favorite memories of Dipa Ma is from the early seventies when I and many of my friends were living in India, practicing meditation quite ardently. One of my friends received a letter from his mother, who was furious that he was there in India practicing Buddhism. She said, "I would rather see you in hell than where you are now." He was pretty shocked and couldn't imagine how to respond. He told Dipa Ma about the situation, and whenever he saw Dipa Ma after that, she would ask him, "How is your mother? Is she feeling better? When you meditate, do you send her lovingkindness?" Later, Dipa Ma gave my friend a hundred-rupee note, which a student had given to her as a donation. At that time the note was worth about twelve dollars, which was a lot of money for Dipa Ma. She gave it to him, saying, "Go buy a present and send it to your mother." One of the Buddha's teachings suggests that if you are angry with someone, you should give them a gift. That two-thousand-year-old teaching suddenly came alive for my friend in the form of this woman, who had so little herself, providing the money for her student to make a gesture of reconciliation.

I remember Dipa Ma not only as my teacher but as a woman, and a mother, and a grandmother. Once, someone asked her if she found her worldly concerns a hindrance. She said, "They are not a hindrance because whatever I do, the meditation is there. It never really leaves me. Even when I am talking, I am meditating. When I am eating or thinking about my daughter—this does not hinder the meditation." When she visited the United States with her family, I remember watching her playing games with her young grandson, Rishi, laughing and laughing, and then getting up to instruct someone in meditation. Then, perhaps, she would go wash her clothes by hand and hang them out to dry. She might do walking meditation and then return to the house to sit. Rishi would be running around the room, while Dipa Ma's daughter would be cooking or watching television at a high volume. And Dipa Ma would be meditating right there in the midst of all that. Whenever anyone sat down in front of her, she would open her eyes and shower the person with blessings.

Even though she was barely four feet tall and in frail health, Dipa Ma's energy was powerful. I remember her as a dynamic warrior in practice and a very demanding teacher.

When Joseph Goldstein and I saw her in India not long before she died, she suggested that we try to sit in meditation for two days. She didn't mean a two-day retreat, but two days of nonstop meditating. Both of us were convinced that we weren't capable of doing something like that (and I wonder if she really thought we were). But when we started to protest, she just said, "Don't be lazy."

I still hear her voice whispering to me, challenging me to extend myself to find what I am actually capable of, especially when I feel limited in terms of the amount of love and compassion I can arouse. As with all of us, my capacity for lovingkindness far exceeds my ideas about my capacity. When I find myself hesitating, not going forward and manifesting the connection I am able to, I see an image of her opening her eyes and blessing someone, or offering my friend that money to buy his mother a gift, or I hear her voice telling me, "Don't be lazy." Then I go forward.

For more information

READERS who desire information about Insight Meditation retreats and teaching worldwide may contact the Insight Meditation Society, 1230 Pleasant Street, Barre, Massachusetts 01005. For information about Insight Meditation audio and video cassette recordings, please contact the Dharma Seed Tape Library, Box 66, Wendell Depot, Massachusetts 01380.

Books by Sharon Salzberg

A Heart As Wide As the World:
Stories on the Path of Lovingkindess

The Buddhist teachings have the power to transform our lives for the better, says Sharon Salzberg, and the need to bring about this transformation can be found in the ordinary events of our everyday experiences. Salzberg distills more than twenty-five years of teaching and practicing meditation into a series of short essays, rich with anecdotes and personal revelations, that offer genuine aid and comfort for anyone on the spiritual path.

Lovingkindness: The Revolutionary Art of Happiness

In this inspiring book, Sharon Salzberg shows us how the Buddhist path of lovingkindness can help us discover the radiant, joyful heart within each of us. This practice of lovingkindness is revolutionary because it has the power to radically change our lives, helping us cultivate true happiness in ourselves and genuine compassion for others.

Voices of Insight

In this anthology, leading Western teachers of Buddhism share their personal experiences on the path of insight meditation; their understanding of the basic teachings of the Buddha; the lessons they've learned in their training with their own teachers; and some good advice on following the Buddha Dharma in everyday situations of work, family, and service.